Agile Oracle Application Express

Patrick Cimolini
Karen Cannell

Apress®

Agile Oracle Application Express

ISBN-13 (pbk): 978-1-4302-3759-4

ISBN-13 (electronic): 978-1-4302-3760-0

President and Publisher: Paul Manning
Lead Editor: Jonathan Gennick
Technical Reviewer: Scott Wesley
Editorial Board: Steve Anglin, Ewan Buckingham, Gary Cornell, Louise Corrigan, Morgan Ertel, Jonathan Gennick, Jonathan Hassell, Robert Hutchinson, Michelle Lowman, James Markham, Matthew Moodie, Jeff Olson, Jeffrey Pepper, Douglas Pundick, Ben Renow-Clarke, Dominic Shakeshaft, Gwenan Spearing, Matt Wade, Tom Welsh
Coordinating Editor: Anita Castro
Copy Editor: Tiffany Taylor
Compositor: Bytheway Publishing Services
Indexer: SPI Global
Artist: SPI Global
Cover Designer: Anna Ishchenko

Distributed to the book trade worldwide by Springer Science+Business Media New York, 233 Spring Street, 6th Floor, New York, NY 10013. Phone 1-800-SPRINGER, fax (201) 348-4505, e-mail orders-ny@springer-sbm.com, or visit www.springeronline.com.

For information on translations, please e-mail rights@apress.com, or visit www.apress.com.

Apress and friends of ED books may be purchased in bulk for academic, corporate, or promotional use. eBook versions and licenses are also available for most titles. For more information, reference our Special Bulk Sales–eBook Licensing web page at www.apress.com/bulk-sales.

Any source code or other supplementary materials referenced by the author in this text is available to readers at www.apress.com. For detailed information about how to locate your book's source code, go to www.apress.com/source-code/.

Contents at a Glance

Contents

About the Authors

Patrick Cimolini, P.Eng., PMP, is a principal with Patrick International APEX Consulting, a consultancy specializing in project management and software development services for Oracle Application Express (APEX) projects. Formal training in engineering, business administration, and project management is complemented by 30 years of experience that has evolved through mainframe, client/server, and web platforms. Patrick enjoys attending the Oracle Development Tools User Group (ODTUG) conferences where he has been a regular presenter.

Karen Cannell is president of TH Technologies, a small consulting firm providing Oracle technology services, lately focused on Application Express. A mechanical engineer by degree (one of them), she has analyzed, designed, developed, converted, upgraded, enhanced, and otherwise worked on legacy and commercial database applications for more than 25 years, concentrating on Oracle technologies since 1994. Karen has worked with Application Express since its Web DB and HTMLDB beginnings, and continues to leverage the Oracle suite of tools to build quality web applications for clients in government, medical, and engineering industries. Karen may be contacted at kcannell@thtechnology.com.

About the Technical Reviewer

 **Scott Wesley** is a database consultant and trainer with the Sage Computing Services team. Since joining the industry at the turn of the century, he has gained analyst programming experience in a wide variety of applications within retail, government, and financial sectors, predominantly using PL/SQL, Oracle Forms, and, more recently, Oracle Application Express.

Scott actively researches and applies cutting-edge technologies from the Oracle product range and is keenly interested in researching and sharing product knowledge on underutilized database-level functionality.

Occasionally you'll find Scott in the OTN forums, AskTom, PL/SQL Challenge, or helping with Australian Oracle User Group (AUSOUG) events. He also blogs occasionally at `http://triangle-circle-square.blogspot.com` and has side interests in science and skepticism.

Acknowledgments

The following friends, colleagues, and mentors have influenced my thinking and made me a better person: John Root, Larry Hick, Larry Burns, Jack Mears, the late Dr. Norbert Berkowitz, and Jack Stephenson, to name a few. A big thank you goes to April Bending, my wife, who supported and encouraged me to take a big step out of my comfort zone.

Patrick Cimolini

Many thanks to Jon Eskesen, Russ Boekenkroger, and Robert Reidman, who gave me the opportunity to do more that I thought I could. I also extend thanks to all my colleagues through the years, who have taught me much about working together, working styles, and getting things done.

Special thanks to Gary and Kali, who tolerate my brain on APEX.

Karen Cannell

Introduction

Yogi Berra once said, *"It's easy to get good players. Getting 'em to play together, that's the hard part."* Since you are reading this book, I am assuming you are already a skilled computer professional who is motivated to look for better ways of delivering high-value software to your customers. In other words, you are already a *"good player."* This book's central theme speaks to Yogi's *"hard part"*: getting good players to play together.

To build a winning team, a coach needs good players, good equipment, and good plays. In the software development industry, the players are software developers who have a passion for building software systems and applications that deliver high value to their customers. Motivated software developers spend a significant amount of their personal time honing their existing skills and learning new ones. Oracle Application Express (APEX) is an excellent piece of equipment. In the hands of a skilled professional team, APEX is used to quickly build web applications that sit on top of an Oracle database. APEX is a seriously practical Rapid Application Development (RAD) tool. Agile Software Development is, for the software industry, an effective and lightweight playbook. The Agile Manifesto and its 12 underlying principles define a practical strategy for enabling software development teams to get valuable and stable software to the customer within a short time frame. APEX and Agile are a winning combination.

APEX and Agile are complementary. They fit together like a hand in a glove. This book's goal is to show you how the APEX tool and the Agile process work together. Both emphasize rapid delivery of software. APEX's efficient declarative software development environment enables software developers to live up to the Agile principle, *"working software is delivered frequently."* APEX's Team Development module, especially its feedback mechanism, encourages and facilitates interaction among all stakeholders. Interaction among stakeholders is a core Agile value.

Using APEX and Agile together will energize you and your team, make you more productive, and will help you to soften Yogi's *"hard part."*

CHAPTER 1

Agile Software Development

Before Oracle Application Express (APEX) can be discussed in the light of Agile software development, the stage must be set by defining, for the purposes of this book, what is meant by Agile software development.

This chapter introduces you to the core principles of Agile software development. The core principles were developed by the team of leading software developers who created the Agile Alliance in 2011. The core principles are expressed in the *Agile Manifesto,* which is further supported by *The Twelve Principles of Agile Software;* the up-to-date versions of these very short and concise principles can be found at the Agile Alliance web site (www.AgileAlliance.org). These core principles are the common ground that is shared by a number of lightweight software development methodologies. These methodologies grew up and evolved during the latter part of the twentieth century. Some of the common lightweight methodologies are summarized in this chapter because they are useful in the APEX context.

An in-depth discussion of Agile software development is beyond the scope of this book; however, you will leave this chapter with a solid overview of Agile software development. The rest of the book shows how APEX can be configured to directly support the core principles of Agile software development, turning groups of highly skilled and motivated individual developers into effective teams that lead their organizations to technical, strategic, and commercial success.

Agile History

In February 2001, 17 seasoned senior software developers met in Snowbird, Utah. These developers shared a passion for finding better ways of building software and a passion for sharing their thoughts and methodologies with the software development community. The meeting's goal was to find and articulate the common principles, if any, that underpin the various lightweight software development methodologies that the group had been using to manage their software development projects.

The lightweight software development methodologies were conceived, born, and nurtured because the group was frustrated with the classic engineering and project management approaches to software development. The classic approaches often failed, some with spectacularly embarrassing and very public negative results.

The Snowbird meeting produced four significant results:

- The word *Agile*

- The Agile Manifesto

- The Twelve Principles of Agile Software

- The Agile Alliance

The Word Agile

The word Agile was an important result from the Snowbird meeting. It effectively branded the software industry's intuitive movement toward lightweight project governance processes that embrace an iterative approach to discovering what a finished software product should do and look like.

The branding step was highly successful. One Snowbird participant, Alistair Cockburn, observed that an Agile conference was held within six months of the initial Snowbird meeting. Now the word *Agile*, in the context of software development, has become synonymous with the phrase *Agile software development*. Agile refers to the core concepts that are shared by all of the lightweight software development methodologies.

Agile Manifesto

The current version of the Agile Manifesto is (www.AgileAlliance.org) as follows:

> *We are uncovering better ways of developing software by doing it and helping others do it. Through this work we have come to value:*
>
> *Individuals and interactions ....over processes and tools*
> *Working software ....over comprehensive documentation*
> *Customer collaboration ....over contract negotiation*
> *Responding to change ....over following a plan*
> *That is, while there is value in the items on the right, we value the items on the left more.*

The Snowbird group, despite the strong commitment of individual members to individual lightweight methodologies, quickly found this common ground.

The Agile Manifesto itself is a shining example of the Agile core principles. It is concise; it says much in a few words. It is lightweight, effective, and sufficient.

The first sentence celebrates the Snowbird group's altruistic commitment to the software industry. The four values distill software development into four core activities. The concluding statement is important because it explicitly states that while the group values a lightweight approach to software development, software development governance can never be zero-weight. The items on the right do have value and play an important part in building software. Without the items on the right, software development falls into the hellish abyss of endless, undisciplined hacking and cowboy coding.

The Twelve Principles of Agile Software

The current version of the Agile Manifesto's Twelve Principles of Agile Software is as follows (www.AgileAlliance.org):

- *Our highest priority is to satisfy the customer through early and continuous delivery of valuable software.*

- *Welcome changing requirements, even late in development. Agile processes harness change for the customer's competitive advantage.*

- *Deliver working software frequently, from a couple of weeks to a couple of months, with a preference to the shorter timescale.*

- *Working software is the primary measure of progress.*

- *Agile processes promote sustainable development. The sponsors, developers, and users should be able to maintain a constant pace indefinitely.*

- *Close, daily co-operation between business people and developers*

- *The most efficient and effective method of conveying information to and within a development team is face-to-face conversation.*

- *Build projects around motivated individuals. Give them the environment and support they need, and trust them to get the job done.*

- *Continuous attention to technical excellence and good design enhances agility.*

- *Simplicity—the art of maximizing the amount of work not done—is essential.*

- *The best architectures, requirements, and designs emerge from self-organizing teams.*

- *At regular intervals, the team reflects on how to become more effective, then tunes and adjusts its behavior accordingly.*

The Snowbird group felt that the Agile Manifesto required some clarifying points. After a long day, the group agreed on the Twelve Principles of Agile Software. The principles start to give concrete direction to how the Agile Manifesto can be applied.

The Agile Alliance

The Agile Alliance describes itself as follows:

> . . . *a nonprofit organization with global membership, committed to advancing Agile development principles and practices. We believe that Agile approaches deliver higher value faster, and make the software industry more productive, humane, and sustainable.*

You can delve into the Agile Alliance's offerings at www.agilealliance.org. The Agile Alliance is a hotbed of inspiration. The web site contains the most recent versions of the Agile Manifesto and its Twelve Principles of Agile Software. The web site acts as an international hub for the Agile community. Membership gives you access to a wide variety of resources that include an article library, videos, presentations, local user group listings, and links to additional Agile resources. The Agile Alliance organizes an annual conference, where you can attend presentations and network with the leading proponents of Agile. The Agile Alliance also provides financial and organizational support to scores of local, regional, and international special interest conferences and user groups. For anyone interested in Agile, it is an ideal starting point.

Agile Software Development Methodologies

While the individuals in the Snowbird group agreed on the Agile Manifesto and its Twelve Principles of Agile Software, they agreed to disagree on what methodologies are appropriate for applying the Manifesto and Principles to work on the shop floor. The disagreement recognizes that a single, one-size-fits-all methodology that is universally applicable in all situations will never be found. This is probably a wise conclusion.

The following sections outline the high-level features of some of the key lightweight methodologies. There are books devoted to each methodology that take great pains to describe their inner workings. This discussion limits itself to only the methodology features that are useful in the context of APEX and its relationship with Agile.

All of the methodologies support the Agile Manifesto and its Twelve Principles of Agile Software. Therefore, it is not surprising to find that there is a great deal of overlap between the methodologies. The methodologies differ in terminology and the emphasis that they put on the various Agile approaches, tools, and techniques.

Adaptive Software Development (ASD)

Adaptive software development (ASD) grew out of rapid application development (RAD) work by Jim Highsmith, one of the Snowbird group, and Sam Bayer.

This methodology gives us a key insight; an explicit recognition that stakeholders do not know everything about a problem at hand and have probably made some false assumptions about the problem. The lack of knowledge and erroneous assumptions are corrected by using an iterative series of speculate, collaborate, and learn cycles. The word *speculate* is used in place of planning; this recognizes the uncertainty involved building an accurate model of a business problem. The word *collaboration* pays homage to the open and frank communication between all of the stakeholders. The word *learn* describes short, time-boxed development iterations that include design, build, and testing. The learn cycle allows the extended team to learn and quickly adapt the solution based on real working software. Thus, the team acquires a deeper understanding of the problem and is able to correct false assumptions and to fix outright mistakes in the original specification.

ASD uses the following terminology to describe its life cycle: mission-focused, feature-based, iterative, time-boxed, risk-driven, and change-tolerant.

Extreme Programming (XP)

Extreme programming (XP) is a software development methodology that takes some software development best practices to extreme levels. Its key features are time-boxing, paired programming, test-driven development, coding features only when they are required, flat management structure, simplicity and clarity in the code, expecting requirement changes, and frequent communication with customers and fellow programmers.

The term extreme is used because the methodology is intolerant of activities that do not produce useful results immediately. For example, adding a column to a table because it will be useful in the future is not done. The future column is not added because it adds cost and complication today with no off-setting benefit. There is also a significant risk that the future column might never be required. The extreme strategy is to add the column only when it is, in fact, required.

Scrum

Scrum is an iterative, incremental framework for project management. It was originally conceived for managing product development and was adopted by the software development industry.

The word scrum, in the context of rugby, describes a play where the entire team interlocks their arms and pushes as a single unit with the aim of getting control of the ball. This analogy of aggressive and cooperative teamwork has attraction for software developers.

The word scrum refers to the daily stand-up meeting where the day's immediate work is planned. The daily scrum meeting is held at the same time and in the same place. It starts on time and ends on time after 15 minutes. Anyone can sit in on the meeting, but only the direct team members speak. The team members briefly summarize what was accomplished on the previous day and what will be accomplished on the coming day, and raise a flag if they are experiencing a problem. Problem resolution is done after the meeting. This meeting style keeps all members accountable for their work and gets individual problems resolved quickly.

Work is done in time-boxed sprints that last approximately two to four weeks. In this context, the word time-box implies a hard deadline. Working software is always released to the test or acceptance teams exactly on schedule. If some software features run behind schedule, they are removed from the sprint and put back into the backlog list, where they can be included in a later sprint.

Sprints are controlled through three meetings:

- *Planning.* The sprint planning meeting brings the team together with the product owner. The meeting's output is a list of features that will be included in the sprint.

- *Technical review.* A sprint review meeting is held at the end of a sprint. The meeting looks at the work that was completed and the work that was not completed. The completed work is demonstrated to the stakeholders.

- *Process review.* A sprint retrospective meeting is also held at the end of a sprint. This meeting is the team's "lessons learned" exercise. In this meeting, the team reviews the sprint from a process perspective: what worked, what failed, how can the next sprint be improved.

All scrum meetings require strict discipline; they are time-boxed and must stick to the agenda. The central management artifacts that organize scrum work are the product backlog and the sprint backlog.

- *Product backlog.* The product backlog is a list of high-level features that describe the product that is under construction.

- *Sprint backlog.* The sprint backlog is a list of tasks that are required to build the items in the product backlog. During a sprint, individual programmers or programmer pairs check out the sprint backlog items, code them, and then mark them as completed. The check-out process occurs in the context of the daily scrum, where the team members check out sprint backlog items in an open and transparent manner, which fosters a spirit of teamwork and camaraderie.

The scrum's management structure is flat and has a limited number of roles. The scrum master is the team's project manager or team lead. The team consists of up to seven or eight cross-functional team members. The product owner represents the customer stakeholders.

Crystal

Crystal is a family of related methodologies. The families are color-coded as clear, yellow, orange, and red. The colors darken as projects grow in size and more programmers are added to the team; thus more governance artifacts are added as the project size increases. A second dimension deals with the cost of failure. If failure costs are high, then more quality-assurance rigor and formality are added to the development process.

Crystal values people and community over processes and tools. While the processes and tools are important, they exist only to support the people who are the critical success factor in software development. Crystal is also tolerant of different software development cultures. It encourages teams to pick and choose between the various Agile tools and processes in order to select the right mix for the project at hand.

Within the Crystal culture of tolerance, there are, however, two rules that are common to all of the colors: projects must use incremental development with increments of four months or less, and the team must hold reflection workshops before and after each increment.

The author of Crystal, Alistair Cockburn, notes that successful teams are concerned with the properties of a successful project and choose processes and tools that will ensure that their projects acquire these properties. The properties are as follows:

- Frequent delivery

- Reflective improvement

- Close/osmotic communication

- Personal safety

- Focus

- Easy access to expert users

- Technical environment with automated tests, configuration management, and frequent integration

- Collaboration across organizational boundaries

Feature-Driven Development (FDD)

Feature-driven development (FDD) is model-centric. FDD focuses on building a high-level model of a problem solution before coding begins. The model consists of a list of features that are visible and important to the client. The features are broken down into pieces that can be coded and delivered within short development cycles, typically two weeks.

Five core activities make up FDD. They are as follows:

- Develop overall model

- Build feature list

- Plan by feature

- Design by feature

- Build by feature

Progress is tracked by milestones and an easy-to-implement method of tracking percentage complete for both individual features and the overall project.

Dynamic System Development Method (DSDM)

The Dynamic System Development Method (DSDM) was born in the United Kingdom in the early 1990s. DSDM is a more mature and disciplined version of rapid application development (RAD). Over the last two decades, DSDM has been guided by the DSDM Consortium. The Consortium has published a number of DSDM revisions that have evolved in parallel with Agile, and DSDM continues to evolve.

DSDM combines formal project management structures with iterative development. Projects are divided into three high-level phases. The second phase is further divided into five stages.

- Phase 1: The pre-project

- Phase 2: The project life cycle

- • Feasibility study

- • Business study

- • Functional model iteration

- • Design and build iteration

- • Implementation

- • Phase 3: The post-project

The three phases and the two studies fit nicely into a classic project management view of software development. The modeling, design and build, and implementation stages are divided into iterative efforts that deliver working software on a scheduled basis. The iterative stages are the Agile part of the methodology.

PRAGMATIC PROGRAMMING

You'll sometimes hear the term *pragmatic programming* bandied about as if it referred to a methodology in the same sense as, say, extreme programming. Pragmatic programming is not a formal methodology. Rather, it is a mindset that is used by experienced Agile programmers who assemble individual Agile techniques to build a unique Agile framework for each project.

Unified Processes (UP)

Several lightweight versions of IBM Rational Unified Process (RUP) have achieved traction in the Agile world. They are as follows:

- • Agile Unified Process (AUP)

- • Essential Unified Process (EssUP)

- • Open Unified Process (OpenUP)

Agile Unified Process (AUP) has been described as a methodology that lies somewhere between the formal RUP methodology and the informal extreme programming (XP) methodology.

The Agile UP is based on the following philosophies:

- • *Your staff knows what they're doing*: People are not going to read detailed process documentation, but they will want some high-level guidance and/or training from time to time.

- • *Simplicity*: Everything is described concisely using a handful of pages, not thousands of them.

- • *Agility*: The Agile UP conforms to the values and principles of Agile software development.

- • *Focus on high-value activities*: The focus is on the activities that actually count, not every possible thing that could happen to you on a project.

- *Tool independence*: You can use any toolset that you want with the Agile UP. The recommendation is that you use the tools that are best suited for the job, which are often simple tools.

- *Tailoring*: You'll want to tailor the AUP to meet your own needs.

The Agile Unified Process distinguishes between two types of iterations. A development release iteration results in a deployment to the quality assurance and/or demo area. A production release iteration results in a deployment to the production area.

Essential Unified Process (EssUP) is similar to the Agile Unified Process in that it evolved from the IBM Rational Unified Process. EssUP encourages teams to customize their project governance by picking the practices that suit their environment and tailoring them to their culture.

Open Unified Process (OpenUP) takes advantage of the overall structural aspects of RUP. It discards some of the heavier processes and artifacts and streamlines others. The result is a lightweight, iterative methodology that works within a high-level project plan that lays out the complete project life cycle. The actual work is subdivided into time-boxed iterations that span several weeks. The iterations are further broken down into micro-increments that span hours or days.

Agile and Your Team

The Snowbird group agreed that there is no magic methodology that suits all situations at all times. So how does a team pick the right methodology? The answer can be found by asking a few probing questions:

- How much will failure cost?

- How large is your project?

- What culture exists in your shop?

Cost of Failure

What follows is a true story. In a fluid dynamics engineering class, a student asked the professor how many terms of the Bernoulli equation are typically used in the field. The professor turned from the whiteboard and said, "It depends on how much the screw-up is going to cost you."

The Bernoulli equation can be used to calculate the amount of fluid that flows through a pipe. The equation contains many terms and variations that account for the size of the pipe, the roughness of the pipe's walls, the viscosity of the fluid, etc. The professor's point was that when you are on a construction site and a hole starts filling with water, you can just eyeball the situation and then run down to the nearest equipment rental company and get a submersible pump. Your pump size choices are limited to small, medium, large, and extra large. You make a guess, rent one, throw it in the hole, and see what happens. If the water starts going down, you are finished. If not, go back to the rental company and get another pump. In this scenario, you do not even use the Bernoulli equation; there is no formal analysis or planning as the cost of not getting the right size of pump is minimal. In short, this situation can be managed successfully by an Agile methodology that gets a working solution in place quickly and can be quickly changed based on immediate feedback.

On the other hand, if you are asked to deliver a critical amount of fluid to a process on a space shuttle, the situation changes dramatically. Getting the design wrong is simply not acceptable because the cost is horrific in financial terms and, more importantly, loss of life terms. You cannot correct a problem in the space shuttle by fixing it on the fly. An Agile approach in this case is clearly not an option.

Project governance weight and formality must increase in step with the cost of failure.

Project Size

One criticism of Agile is that it does not scale. This might be a fair observation. A daily 15-minute stand-up meeting does not work for a team of several hundred persons. On the other hand, one anecdote claims that a 10-programmer Agile team succeeded in a short time frame where a 26-programmer team that used a heavy project governance failed over a period of several years. Team efficiency must be factored into the conversation when talking about scalability.

Big projects can be subdivided so that smaller teams can apply Agile to their work. This is also a reasonable strategy with the caveat that inter-team communication must be addressed.

Figure 1-1 is a simplistic illustration that shows the relationship between cost of failure and size against the lightness or heaviness of project governance. As the cost of failure increases, the risk is addressed by putting heavier, more formal project management processes in place.

As project size increases, communication becomes more complicated. Again, the problem is addressed by putting heavier, more formal communication processes in place.

The important observation here, from an Agile perspective, is that the quadrant boundaries are not hard. There are gentle gradations between the highs and lows. Most Agile methodologies recommend an incremental approach to increasing the heaviness of project governance.

Agile's approach strives to follow the Goldilocks principle: do not add too much governance, do not add too little governance, but add just the right amount of governance.

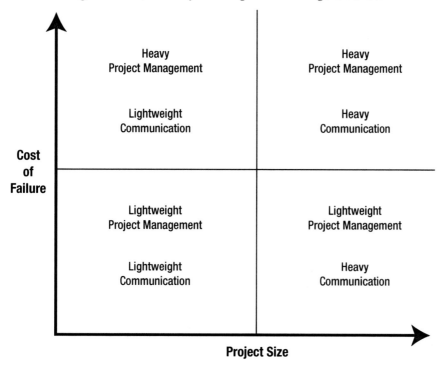

Figure 1-1. Project governance trade-offs

Fitting Agile into Your Culture

Is Agile right for your team? How much governance do you apply?

The answer to the first question is usually "yes." Many teams find that an Agile approach to software development is a natural way to work, even within and despite a formal governance setting. Years ago, I worked on a mid-sized project that started out with a good product description. A formal project plan was formulated, and a big Gantt chart was posted on a wall and regularly updated. The project started and working software was delivered to the client on schedule. The client's vision of the product quickly evolved as a result of seeing and working with the software. Together, the client and development teams found better ways to solve some of the business problems. As a result, the project drifted from following the plan and produced a product that was superior to the planned product. However, the formal governance processes did not adapt. Team members booked hours for actual tasks to planned tasks that were never started. The project management reports became quite useless. In the end, the team paid lip service to the formal project management processes while getting the real work done on the shop floor, using our own home-grown Agile methodology that was iterative and time-boxed. Of course, this was long before the word Agile was introduced to our industry. The lesson learned here is that Agile is a natural way to work and feels "right."

If you decide to adopt Agile, how do you go about getting it up and running in your shop? There are two broad options:

- *Adopt a methodology.* A team can adopt an existing Agile methodology that fits their culture. This approach takes advantage of existing documentation, templates, and possibly an active Agile community for support.

- *Build your own methodology.* Study the Agile Manifesto, and then pick Agile processes and techniques from several of the methodologies to produce a custom Agile solution for your situation.

Some of the individual Agile methodologies have been summarized earlier. The following is a sampling of the Agile processes and techniques that can be assembled into an Agile environment that is unique to a team or project. Most of these processes and techniques are shared among the lightweight methodologies; only the terminology and emphasis change.

- Time boxing

- Expecting requirement changes

- Frequent communication with customers and fellow programmers

- Daily stand-up meetings

- Paired programming

- Side-by-side programming

- Flat management structure

- Easy access to expert personnel

- Focus time

- Reflective learning

- Test-driven development

- Code features only when they are required

- Simplicity and clarity in the code

When you adopt Agile, how much governance do you apply to your projects? The answer is never crystal clear. Figure 1-2 helps visualize the approaches.

Zero weight is never an option. All projects, no matter how small, need some governance or they quickly degrade into costly chaos. In my own work on small projects where I am the only programmer, I always work from a written task list that is very terse. It is often written in pencil on a scrap of paper. I do this because of the following:

- Writing the list often uncovers issues that I did not think of.

- The list keeps me on track when I am interrupted in the middle of the work. I check off each task as I complete it so that when I return after an interruption, I pick up exactly where I left off. This keeps me efficient and prevents me from forgetting a step, which causes unnecessary debugging later on.

The main point here is that zero-weight governance has the attraction of zero capital cost; however, its operating cost can be huge.

Lightweight project governance is Agile's sweet spot. As a rule of thumb, your governance should be sufficient and effective. Anything more is a needless cost.

However, there are always valid reasons to adopt a heavyweight governance strategy. Some reasons are as follows:

- High cost of failure

- Large project

- Risk-averse environment

- Existing command and control environment that is entrenched

Where do you draw the line between lightweight and heavyweight project governance? There is no easy answer. The answer will come from open, frank, and sometimes tense communication between the stakeholders.

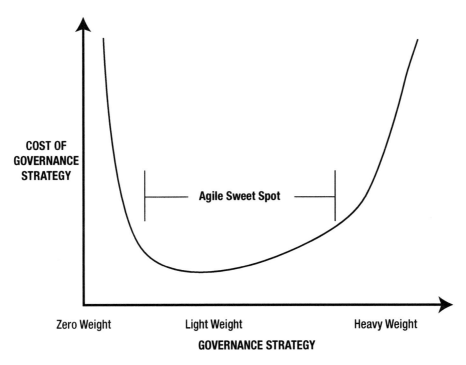

Figure 1-2. The cost of governance strategies

Tools, Process, People

Organizing your work environment involves three important areas: tools, process, and people. Figure 1-3 points out that the critical success factor is the people. It is easy to lose sight of this observation in the software development industry. We are constantly bombarded with aggressive advertising and sales calls from software and hardware vendors who claim that their tools will boost our productivity. There are many strident schools and institutes that promote their processes and methodologies as the key to hitting our cost, schedule, and quality targets. In order to work efficiently, people do need tools and process; however, tools and process are useless without good people. In Agile terms, this observation becomes as follows:

That is, while there is value in tools and process, we value people more.

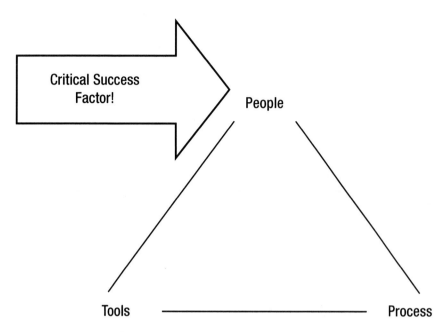

Figure 1-3. The artifacts that keep your work environment organized

Summary

This chapter is a lightweight introduction to Agile. The chapter has introduced the Agile Manifesto, its Twelve Principles of Agile Software, individual Agile methodologies, and some of the key Agile processes and techniques. For in-depth insights, go to the Agile Alliance web site at www.AgileAlliance.org or Google the keywords that were introduced earlier.

Is Agile a panacea? No! Software development is an inherently messy activity. No tool, process, or methodology will ever completely sanitize it. Developing software has a lot in common with playing a contact sport like football or rugby. The individual players work hard to develop their game skills. The team management buys the best equipment it can afford. The coaches devise plays and drill the players on play execution. Then, on game day, contact happens, it rains, it snows, the opposition is bigger and faster, plays go well, plays go badly, and the team scrambles to adjust to ever-changing conditions. At the end of the game, the team comes off the field, tired, limping, battered, bruised, bloodied, and laughing about all the fun they had.

CHAPTER 2

Agile and APEX

Delivery of high-quality working software to users on a fast and regular basis is a key goal of Agile software development. Oracle Application Express is a highly efficient rapid application development (RAD) environment. Therefore, it is not surprising that these two entities dovetail together extremely well.

This chapter steps through the Agile Manifesto with its Twelve Principles of Agile Software and highlights the areas where APEX supports Agile software development. The goal of this chapter is to give you insights into how you and your team (the people) can use Agile software development (the process) together with APEX (the tool) in ways that will enable you to reap the incredible commercial benefits that are inherent in these complementary environments.

The Agile Manifesto

The Agile Manifesto is short, simple, to the point, and incredibly wise. APEX can be viewed in a similar fashion. APEX's declarative environment and simple underlying architecture make many routine software development tasks short, simple, to the point, and robust.

Individuals and Interactions Over Processes and Tools

Agile software development is a process. It is ironic, but noteworthy too, that the authors of the Agile Manifesto value individuals and interactions more than their brainchild, the process of Agile software development (see Figure 2.1).

Agile software development supports individuals and interactions by promoting a strategic set of processes that fit well with the natural way in which people work. The Agile processes are lightweight and require a minimum of bookkeeping and bureaucracy. This strategy gives developers more time for producing working software.

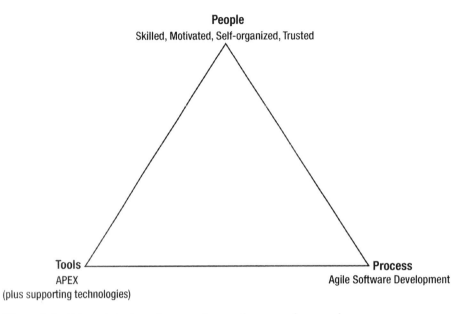

People
Skilled, Motivated, Self-organized, Trusted

Tools
APEX
(plus supporting technologies)

Process
Agile Software Development

Figure 2-1. Although tools and process have value, we value people more.

APEX supports individuals and interactions by providing a set of tools that are lightweight and supportive of both individual work effort and team collaboration.

APEX wizards are one of the chief tools that support an individual developer. There are wizards that help you create most of the artifacts in APEX. Each wizard guides you through a set of pages that contain related properties. In this way, you create an artifact by entering data for the 20% of the properties that do 80% of your work. This method is far more humane and efficient than going to a single page that has all of the artifact's properties. The single page with all the properties can be confusing because the important 20% of the items are mixed in with the 80% that are rarely used. It is easy to miss an important property, which means you must return to the artifact later to debug what you missed.

APEX's Team Development module supports team collaboration. Team Development provides a light but rich framework that allows a skilled, motivated, and trusted team to self-organize. The feedback mechanism, features, to-dos, bugs, and milestones are used in concert by the team to efficiently and effectively communicate among themselves and outside stakeholders. Team Development is designed so that it is relatively easy for developers to keep it up to date in near real-time. Chapter 6 discusses this important APEX module in detail.

Working Software Over Comprehensive Documentation

Software developers produce working software; that is our primary job. Everything else merely supports the primary purpose and must be looked at as overhead. The overhead is always necessary, but it must be ruthlessly minimized and must never, ever become an end in itself.

APEX's declarative environment is the tool's main mechanism for producing working software. Most of the underlying tough coding is taken care of by the APEX engine. Developers rarely, if ever, have to worry about routine things like record inserts, deletes, and updates. The APEX engine does an excellent job of making these database actions safe, quick, and reliable. The safety, quickness, and reliability stem from three sources: the APEX team, the APEX team's processes, and the tool used to create APEX.

Over the years, I have attended numerous conferences where the APEX team has presented technical papers on APEX. The formal presentations together with informal networking have clearly demonstrated that the APEX team has all the right stuff; they are highly skilled and motivated. They are an embodiment of the Agile Manifesto's opening phrase, "We are uncovering better ways of developing software by doing it and helping others do it."

The APEX team used the Team Development module to manage the construction of APEX 4.0 and continues to use it for the following releases. This fact shows that the team has a good handle on Agile software development processes.

■ **Note** In my opinion, one of the main reasons that APEX produces working software safely and reliably is that it is written in PL/SQL, the Oracle database scripting language. PL/SQL is an old technology; it was added as a database feature in Oracle 6, which was released in 1991. It is now over 20 years old and has matured through many cycles of testing, debugging, and aggressive optimization. It is now extremely stable. Upon this rock, APEX was built.

Working software needs documentation. Documentation has value. This is true because no matter how hard software developers work to make the GUI easy to use and intuitive, there are always some parts that need explanation. This is true for both the external interface that is exposed to the end users and the internal code that the developers must understand in order to do maintenance work.

APEX provides hooks that enable developers to document all aspects of their work in the immediate context of the APEX Application Builder without resorting to weighty three-ring binders full of outdated paper. Websheets, team development, APEX utilities, and the help text features can be used in concert to efficiently produce practical and agile documentation within the APEX context. Chapter 8 covers Agile APEX documentation in detail.

Customer Collaboration Over Contract Negotiation

Customer collaboration that is ongoing throughout a product's development is imperative if the product is to be practical and useful. One of the critical success factors of a software project is customer buy-in. Buy-in is almost always the result of positive collaboration with the development team.

APEX fosters customer collaboration through

- Fast delivery of working software

- Feedback

APEX delivers working software to the customer quickly. This enables the customer to start working with the product to test, debug, and evaluate the requirements.

The feedback mechanism that is built into the APEX Team Development module is an ideal collaboration tool. It enables the customer to provide immediate and useful comments to the development team from within the context of the application. The feedback mechanism is embedded into every page in an APEX application. A customer who sees a bug or thinks of a design change can immediately capture the thought in the feedback page. The customer's comment is captured together with all the underlying details, such as the APEX session state, the customer's browser type and version, the customer's computer operating system, and other data that is often invaluable to the developers.

This cuts out the need for longwinded e-mails that require a sluggish back-and-forth set of questions and answers. Chapter 6 comments on the feedback mechanism in detail.

APEX is not a contract-management system; however, the Feature mechanism in APEX's Team Development module can be used to produce a high-level list of features that contains the start date, due date, and estimated effort in hours (see Figure 2-2). The features can be used as an input into the statement of work, which is a key component of the contract. Chapter 6 discusses the feature mechanism in detail.

Figure 2-2. APEX features can be used in a contract's statement of work.

Responding to Change Over Following a Plan

Change is a fact of life. We are always living in a state of flux, and software development is no exception. Agile software development deals with change by expecting it and planning for it. It does this by putting working software into the customer's hands as quickly as possible so that the team can iterate, multiple times if required, through these stages:

1. Design

2. Build

3. Evaluate

If you have a good understanding of the requirements and a good design, then why iterate through these steps? There are two primary reasons:

> *Bugs:* Bugs are typically associated with the software; software bugs are fixed to make the software conform to the requirements and design. Bugs can also be associated with the requirements and the design; this type of bug can be scary because it can potentially involve a tremendous amount of rework. Delivering working software early is the only way to uncover requirement and design bugs that have not been identified during reviews of the requirements and design.

> *Knowledge transfer:* During a project, the business users constantly learn more and more about the technology; the programmers constantly learn more and more about the business (see Figure 2-3). Knowledge transfer often causes "ah-hah" moments when someone on the team sees a much better solution to a business or technical problem. Planning for change allows the team to take advantage of these "ah-hah" moments to increase the quality of the end product. Sometimes the good ideas can come very close to the end of the project.

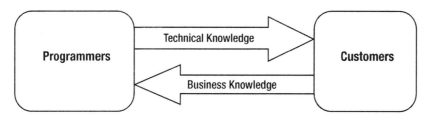

Figure 2-3. Knowledge transfer continues throughout the entire project.

How do you plan for change? You start with a high-level overview of the project. Senior resources look at the initial requirements and sketch in the major entities to form the initial design. Time estimates are the product of expert judgement and must account for the confidence that the team has in the requirements. The team estimates the time required to build the initial version of a module, and then a line item for change is added as a contingency. The team must be careful with this line item: programmers must not view it as a chunk of time to clean up sloppy code—adding error traps and global constants, for example. The initial production code must never be sloppy. The line item for change is reserved strictly for refactoring the product based on legitimate and knowledgeable feedback from the customer.

I recently attended a seminar given by a respected scrum master. The scrum master said that the correct answer from a programmer when asked how long an individual task will take is, "I don't know." This is scary when you are estimating the effort needed to complete a project, especially when a fixed-price contract will govern the work. Solving this dilemma requires expert judgment by senior personnel who can look at a high-level design and assign qualitative descriptions such as *easy, medium*, and *hard* to each entity. Quantitative units of measures, such as hours, are then assigned to the terms *easy, medium*, and *hard* to arrive at the final estimate. The quantitative units of measure are, in turn, affected by the computing environment and the skill levels of the available resources. As a project unfolds, you will come in under budget on some entities and over budget on others. The individual unders and overs usually average out if the initial quantitative estimates are reasonable. In other words, your overall estimate can be reasonably accurate even when estimates of individual line items are not precise.

How does APEX support responding to change and building a plan? First, APEX is an efficient rapid application development (RAD) environment. A RAD environment enables you to quickly build the initial version of the application. This environment also enables you to quickly delete a page and then re-create it. Second, the Team Development module can be used to build your initial plan and then evolve with changes as they occur. Chapter 6 discusses Team Development in detail.

The Twelve Principles of Agile Software

Agile's Twelve Principles of Agile Software serve as stepping-stones between the somewhat abstract core values of the Agile Manifesto and the concrete world of software development methodologies. The Twelve Principles give developers a sense of how they can go about applying the Agile Manifesto's values to the real world without getting into the details of the individual Agile methodologies. This section lists the Twelve Principles and points out the features of APEX that support them.

Remember that APEX's primary function is to build a web-based graphical user interface (GUI) on top of an Oracle Relational Database Management System (RDBMS). The following discussion assumes that the database has been constructed and that it is relatively stable. In most cases, end users are content with a high-level overview of the database design; they generally need this information to help them understand the hows and whys of APEX GUI construction. End users are very interested in how their data is displayed so that they quickly get the information they need and clearly see what they must do in order to get their work done. The desire to see information instead of data, and the desire to quickly and intuitively step through workflows, drive a GUI through many iterations of

1. Analyze

2. Design

3. Build

4. Evaluate

The iterative cycles, over time, tend to become shorter as the development team learns the business and the business team learns the technology. In baseball terms, the teams start hitting more and more home runs as the game unfolds.

Customer Satisfaction by Rapid Delivery of Useful Software

From a customer's point of view, software development looks somewhat like building a house. The customer first signs off on the architectural drawings. Then construction begins with lots of visible activity like digging the foundation, pouring the foundation, erecting the walls, and putting on the roof. These activities are highly visible and give the customer a concrete sense of progress. However, once the shell is built, it seems to take forever to reach the move-in date. The finishing work like plumbing, wiring, drywall finishing, and painting must all be completed before the customer can move in. The customer feels frustrated because no big and highly visible tasks are being completed. APEX software development is similar to building a house in that building the shell gives the customer a sense of rapid progress. The comparison breaks down during the finishing stage because in an APEX software development environment, the customer can start using parts of the application in production before the entire application is completed. In other words, they can move into the ground floor while the upper floor is still being finished; there is no paint smell or plaster dust to deal with.

APEX delivers useful software rapidly because it delivers a truly RAD environment. A typical delivery plan can include the following artifacts in quick succession:

- High-level navigation shell

- Administration pages

- Features/Modules

APEX's simple architecture is another major reason that working software is delivered quickly. The architecture enables an application's promotion from the development environment to the test and production environments to be automated. Typically, the promotion effort consumes much less than an hour. Application promotion is a low-risk activity that can be quickly done on a daily or weekly basis.

Note The technical details, tip, tricks, and insights for promoting APEX applications between environments are found in *Pro Oracle Application Express 4* by Tim Fox, John Scott, and Scott Spendolini (Apress, 2011) and *Expert Oracle Application Express* by Dietmar Aust et al. (Apress, 2011).

High-Level Navigation Shell

APEX uses lists and tabs to build the high-level navigation shell that knits the application together (see Figure 2-4). Buttons and report links are used for finer-grained navigation to the lower-level, more-detailed features.

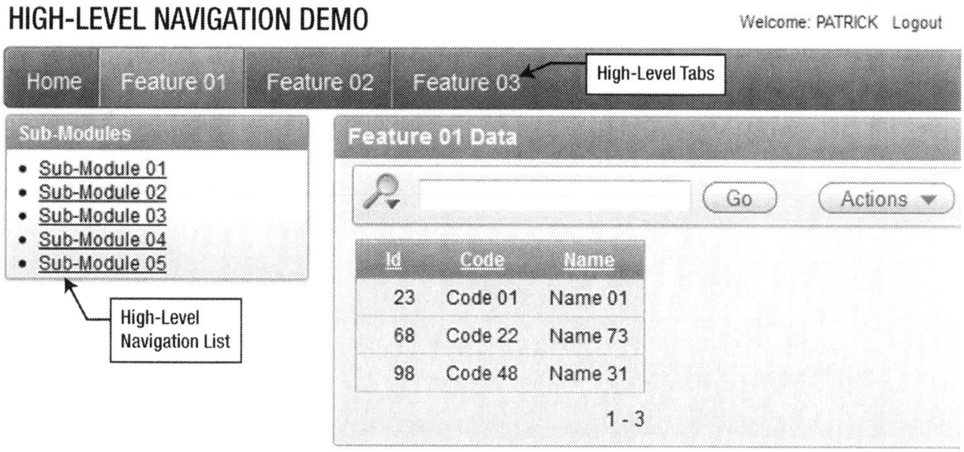

Figure 2-4. High-level navigation shell

The high-level navigation shell takes only a few minutes to create, yet it has a great deal of value to the business users when it is delivered early. The navigation shell gives the business users their first hands-on experience with the application. It is the first concrete step in validating the requirements and design.

Business users and developers often have different visions as to how the requirements and design are translated into working software. The navigation shell is a great starting point to make sure the two visions come together in a spirit of collaboration. The shell is easy to change at this point, so the business users quickly get a sense of ownership when their suggestions appear in the application almost immediately.

The high-level navigation shell is the perfect place to refine terminology. Getting the terminology defined in the users' language at this point enables the developers to use the same terminology in the underlying code as the detailed design and construction unfolds. Agreement between the high-level and low-level terminology is one of the key factors that make an application easier to build, maintain, and document.

■ **Note** At this point, I want to give a word of caution to developers. Developers often trivialize features that are easy to code. Business users can easily be intimidated and feel marginalized when a developer responds to a request with comments and body language that indicates the request is trivial to code. Just because a request is easy to code in the programming domain does not mean that it is trivial in the business domain. Respectful collaboration is a major part of Agile.

Administration Pages

Building an application's administration pages is a great second step after the high-level navigation is in place. The functionality in this area includes application support objects. Lookup tables are a good example. APEX's declarative environment enables the developers to rapidly build the maintenance pages for the support objects. Typically, the maintenance pages are based on tabular forms and interactive reports.

Administrative tabular forms most often are built on top of a single table that has a small number of rows and columns (see Figure 2-5). Building a tabular form on a single table typically takes less than five minutes.

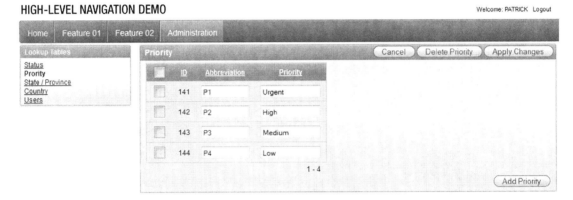

Figure 2-5. Simple tabular form that maintains a lookup table

Interactive reports can also be used to maintain support objects. Interactive reports are generally used for tables that have a large number of rows and require a search function that enables the user to quickly find an individual row or group of related rows (see Figure 2-6). The interactive report page contains links to a page where a new row is created or an existing row is edited (see Figure 2-7). The create and edit functions are both handled by a single APEX page that was created using the form on a table or view wizard. Building an interactive report together with its create and edit supporting page usually takes less than half an hour, assuming the support table has a small number of columns and no complicated dependencies.

Figure 2-6. Simple interactive report that maintains a wide lookup table with many rows

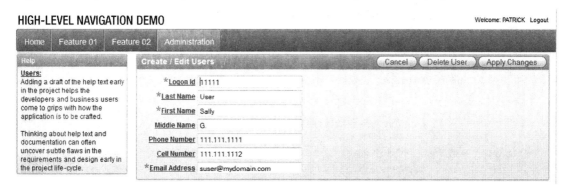

Figure 2-7. Simple form on a table that maintains a row in a wide lookup table

The main point here is that APEX is used to rapidly deliver useful working software to the customer. The customer quickly learns how to work with tabular forms, interactive reports, and data-entry pages in a small, simple, and straightforward environment. As the customer enters the support data, the developers start to learn and absorb the customer's business terminology and get a sense of how the business operates. Two important things happen at this stage of development: an important piece of production code is delivered rapidly, and the two-way knowledge transfer between customer and developer begins in earnest.

Features/Modules

Agile's iterative nature exposes itself when the features are built. At the beginning of this phase of the project plan, the feature designs are still at a relatively high level. The high-level design was adequate for developing the schedule and budget but lacks the nitty-gritty details.

Each feature is developed by iterating through one or more cycles of

1. Mockup

2. Prototype

3. Build

4. Test

5. Evaluate

The initial schedule and budget is based on the assumption that some features will require only one pass through the cycle; the baseball equivalent is a home run. Other features require multiple passes through the cycle before they can pass a critical evaluation.

The APEX declarative environment supports the prototype, build, and test portions of the cycle. The prototype is the APEX version of the mockup; it is rapidly built by using APEX wizards. The build process involves adding business logic to the application; much of this work is done efficiently by using the APEX wizards. Unit testing concentrates on the business rules, not on the mechanical aspects of transporting data from the screen to the database; the APEX engine is extremely reliable from a mechanical point of view.

Changing Requirements Welcomed, Even Late in Development

Conventional wisdom tells us that changes are expensive when they occur late in a project. The extra expense is required because a large change involves reworking many pages and reports.

The Agile and APEX combination significantly mitigates the cost of major changes that occur near the end of a project (see Figure 2-8). The cost mitigation is due to a number of Agile and APEX features:

- Agile's emphasis on close collaboration delivers significant knowledge transfer between the development and business teams. The development team's business knowledge enables them to code solutions quickly without having to pester the business team with lengthy questions and then wait for answers. The flip side of the coin applies to the business team. Their technical knowledge allows them to quickly and accurately communicate with the developers; late in the development process, they have a good idea of what the technology can and cannot do. The two-way knowledge transfer speeds the process of designing and implementing a change, even when the change is complex.

- APEX's RAD environment is just as efficient in delivering changes as it is in delivering the initial application. I recently worked on an APEX project where the sponsor expressed a concern that the development team was spending too little time fixing defects and adding enhancements to a production application. The development team was delivering the changes on time but well under budget, a situation that the sponsor had trouble understanding because of a lifetime of experience where software projects were always late and over budget. In this case, the highly skilled and motivated development team delivered quality code on time and under budget by using a productive tool (APEX) and an effective process (Agile).

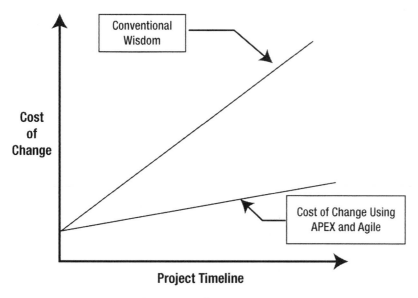

Figure 2-8. *Conceptual illustration of the relative costs of change late in a project*

Working Software Is Delivered Frequently

APEX directly supports the principle of delivering working software frequently by

- Enabling developers to quickly build and modify applications
- Enabling database analysts to easily deploy an application

APEX's declarative environment enables developers to achieve significant results within relatively short development sprints. I have already spoken about APEX's awesome RAD capabilities.

Deploying an application to the test and production environments is a relatively painless and quick process in an APEX environment. The process can be automated so it usually takes less than an hour to deploy an APEX application together with its supporting objects such as JavaScript files and scripts to update the database objects in the parsing schema. The mechanical details for this process are found in the books *Pro Oracle Application Express 4* and *Expert Oracle Application Express* (both Apress, 2011).

Working Software Is the Principle Measure of Progress

The fundamental building block in an APEX environment is a web page. This fact makes it easy and simple to build a public graph that lets everyone know how an APEX project is progressing (see Figure 2-9). A graph that tracks completed pages over time is an effective project health indicator. A project that shows a consistent upward trend in the number of completed pages at the budgeted rate is healthy. An occasional downward blip indicates areas where iterative change has occurred or where significant bugs in the code, design, or requirements were found and corrected. The graph is effective because it is brutally honest.

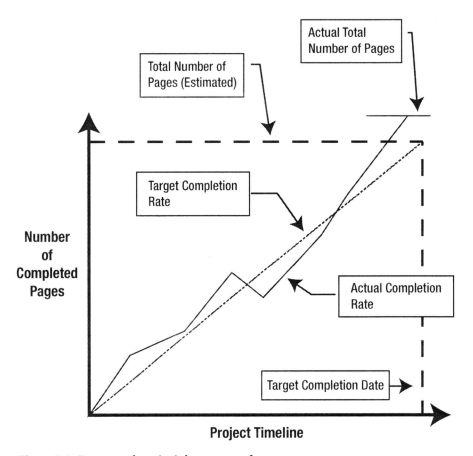

Figure 2-9. Pages are the principle measure of progress.

At the beginning of a project, the total number of pages is estimated. Near the end of the project, the actual total number of pages is added to the graph to illustrate the completion of the project.

This approach of tracking only working pages as the principal measure of progress may seem simplistic to those of you who have been trained in formal project-management practices, where Earned Value Analysis is king. Earned Value Analysis is an elegant way of tracking progress, but it requires a lot of project-management overhead. Tracking working APEX pages is simple, is effective, and requires very little overhead.

Sustainable Development, Able to Maintain a Constant Pace

In the APEX environment, the principle of "sustainable development" is closely related to the principle of "working software is the principle measure of progress." APEX web pages are built quickly by using APEX's declarative tools. As each page is added to an application, it gives the developers a sense of accomplishment; and the customer gets visible proof that progress is being made.

Close, Daily Cooperation Between Business People and Developers

APEX supports the principle of close, daily cooperation between business people and developers through the feedback module that is built into Team Development. This feedback module is discussed in Chapter 6.

Simplicity

Simplicity is an area where APEX shines. APEX's "out of the box" configuration contains very few moving parts (see Figure 2-10). There are only three blocks in the architecture:

- Web browser on the client computer

- Web server

- APEX engine

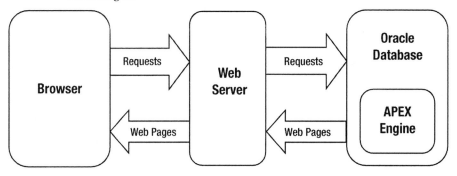

Figure 2-10. *The APEX architecture is simple, with very few moving parts.*

APEX supports most of the common web browsers that are in use today. The user need only enable cookies and JavaScript in their browser of choice. Installation, when required, takes but a few minutes.

The web server handles the two-way communication between the browser and the APEX engine. The web server is responsible for security and file caching. Currently there are three web servers to choose from:

- Oracle HTTP Server (OHS)

- Embedded PL/SQL Gateway (EPG)

- APEX Listener

Choosing the correct web server for your environment is covered in detail in the book *Expert Oracle Application Express* (Apress, 2011). Installing the web server is well documented for both Linux and Windows platforms. Installation and configuration are usually relatively quick and straightforward for experienced operations personnel.

The APEX engine resides inside the Oracle database. It consists of approximately 500 tables and 300 PL/SQL objects such as packages, procedures, and functions. An Oracle database schema named APEX_*xxxxxx* owns the APEX engine, where *xxxxxx* is the APEX version number. This schema is locked; therefore, APEX developers never need to interact with it directly. The APEX engine comes preinstalled in Oracle databases starting with version 9i. Upgrading versions is simple and involves running a few

PL/SQL scripts that are well documented. The book *Expert Oracle Application Express* contains an excellent description of this simple yet powerful and extensible architecture.

Self-Organizing Teams

APEX supports self-organizing teams through its Team Development module. The team has the freedom to plan their sprint activities to the level of detail that suits their development culture. The detailed tasks, called *to-dos* in the Team Development module, can be self-assigned by any developer in the daily morning stand-up meeting. The team is completely free to hit their development targets any way they choose. Team Development allows them to efficiently plan and track who is doing what by when. Chapter 6 covers Team Development in more detail.

Face-to-Face Conversation as the Best Form of Communication

APEX does not explicitly support the principle of face-to-face communication; however, APEX supports the principle implicitly through its approach to documentation. Documentation, when it is created within an Agile and collaborative environment, encourages conversations between the stakeholders. Chapter 8 explores Agile documentation within the APEX context in more detail.

Motivated Individuals Who Are Trusted

Earlier, the chapter spoke about tools, process, and people. People were identified as the critical success factor. I feel strongly that this is true. APEX is not a human resources tool: it does not directly motivate individuals or directly build trust between stakeholders. Indirectly, however, APEX supports motivation and trust by being a good tool that works well. The act of building something that works well is motivating for most developers. Delivering something that works well within a reasonable amount of time builds trust among most stakeholders. APEX, simply by being a good-quality tool, supports both motivation and trust.

Continuous Attention to Technical Excellence

APEX is a tool. It can be used well, or it can be abused. Learning to use APEX well involves two fundamental steps that are true for any tool:

- Read the instructions.

- Hone your skills over time by using the tool and refining your techniques.

The basic instructions that come with APEX are short, concise, and effective. In my experience as a team lead and project manager, I have found that the *2 Day + Application Express Developer's Guide* is all that is required to get a junior programmer up and running with the basics of APEX development.

Expert skill comes later after building a few applications and reading some of the advanced APEX books, such as *Pro Oracle Application Express 4* and *Expert Oracle Application Express* (both Apress, 2011). More important, teams must take techniques from the books and adapt them to the team's environment and technical culture. Chapter 7 suggests a technique for installing a terse and flexible documentation framework for steering your team on a road toward the horizon of technical excellence.

Regular Adaptation to Changing Circumstances

APEX is a tool: an inanimate object that, by itself, cannot adapt to changing circumstances. In the hands of a skilled and motivated developer, it can be an effective instrument of change.

Oracle's APEX development team has set a good example for regularly adapting to change. The team has released major versions of APEX on approximately an annual basis. Each major version has done the following:

- Fixed flaws

- Improved existing features

- Added new features, such as mobile themes, that recognize significant changes in the surrounding environment

APEX itself gives developers the power to change significant aspects of their APEX applications. The theme/template infrastructure enables an APEX team to reconfigure the look and feel of an application dramatically. This is useful in the context of web technology that is rapidly changing as HTML and CSS standards become more mature and user expectations become higher. Plugins allow developers to build their own widgets and interfaces to other systems. APEX plugins have given developers a tool that helps them keep up with changes in their corporate environments.

Summary

APEX is a software-development tool that explicitly complements the Agile software-development processes that are embodied in the Agile Manifesto and its Twelve Principles of Agile Software. Agile values fast delivery of useful software, responsiveness to change, and teamwork. APEX's declarative rapid application development environment supports fast delivery and responsiveness to change. Team Development fosters a spirit of collaboration, cooperation, interdependence, and teamwork across the full spectrum of stakeholders. This winning combination of tool and process leads to the construction of business applications that are successful from both the technical and business perspectives.

CHAPTER 3

Core APEX vs. Enhanced APEX

An important strategic decision must be made at the beginning of an APEX project. The team must decide whether it will use the core APEX product exclusively or whether it will enhance the APEX development environment by adding support technologies that are not built into the APEX framework. This chapter explores the pros and cons of both alternatives so that you can pick your strategy based on all of the considerations. This is not a trivial choice; it has significant impact on all aspects of an APEX project.

Using the core APEX product directly supports two Agile principles, "*customer satisfaction by rapid delivery of useful software*" and "*simplicity*." Using enhanced APEX tends to support the Agile principle of "*continuous attention to technical excellence and good design*." Balancing these two potentially conflicting principles requires intimate knowledge of your software development culture and good judgment.

Strategic Ways Forward

There are four strategic ways forward in an APEX environment. You can do the following:

- Use the core of APEX exclusively

- Enhance APEX with supporting technologies

- Use the core of APEX now and trust that future APEX versions will provide the enhanced functionality that you and your users desire

- Use another technology

Over the last six years, I have had good luck with using the core of APEX exclusively. My users were inside departments, both public and private, and they were content with the default functionality that came with the early versions of HTMLDB and then the newer versions that were rebranded as APEX. My users were, by and large, more interested in getting their applications up and running in production sooner than later; therefore they opted for fast delivery and lower costs over enhanced functionality.

There are legitimate cases, however, in which enhancing the user interface with supporting technologies is highly desirable despite the impact on schedule and cost. One very large client opted to duplicate an existing graphic user interface (GUI) that was built using an older technology. The client felt that the time and cost of building a custom APEX theme and adding some significant JavaScript extensions to APEX was more cost-effective than re-training several thousand users who were scattered around the globe in several different cultures. The project was a success, and the custom theme and the well-crafted JavaScript libraries were reused to great advantage. I believe, however, that much of the JavaScript will be dropped when the client eventually converts the application from APEX 3.2 to APEX 4.x. Another legitimate argument for enhancing APEX with JavaScript technologies is performance.

Moving user interaction logic from the server to the browser reduces the load on the server's CPU and may avoid the cost of an additional CPU license for your Oracle database. Another case for enhancing APEX can be made for applications for which users have very demanding and specific requirements that are not easily supported by the core APEX browser functionality.

If you have patient users, you can develop applications using the core APEX functionality and then wait for newer versions of APEX to supply the desired enhancements. This strategy demands that you aggressively refactor your applications every time you install a new version of APEX to take advantage of its new features.

Occasionally you will run into an application, an environment, or a group of users who need functionality that cannot be satisfied by APEX in a cost-effective manner. In this case, you will need to consider using an alternative technology. However, as APEX matures, the need for this strategy is diminishing.

The following sections explore these strategies in more detail.

Use Core APEX Exclusively

"*Simplicity*" is one of the key principles of Agile software development. Using the core APEX framework exclusively is an elegant way of applying the Agile principle of "*simplicity*" to your development environment. Quickly building useful software that has real value to the customer is another key principle that APEX fully supports with its rapid application development (RAD) environment.

Simplicity and speed stem from APEX's reliance on wizards that walk developers through well-defined declarative steps to create almost all of a web application's components. The APEX Application Builder (see Figure 3-1) makes all of the common components visible at one time. Every component region has a Create button in the upper right corner, which launches the appropriate wizard. In all cases, the wizards create a functional component that works reliably; usually only minor changes are needed after the initial creation. In fact, when the developer takes the time to use the User Interface Defaults to configure the database column attributes, many sub-components like validations are created automatically by the APEX engine. Generally, it takes under a minute to step through a wizard that creates a component.

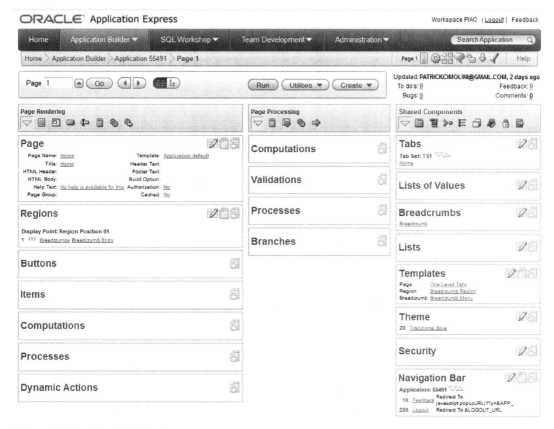

Figure 3-1. *Application Builder*

I have been working with APEX for over six years, and every once in a while I need to step back from the trees to contemplate the forest. Core APEX delivers a lot of useful functionality that experienced APEX developers tend to take for granted. I, for one, must remind myself periodically of the bad old days when I had to write a lot of code to get simple things to work when I worked with other technologies. Core APEX eliminates almost all of the coding that is required to connect a GUI to a database; therefore you free up time for more important things like coding an application's business rules.

Six years ago, my team and I tried to document all of the possible options and permutations that are created when you mix and match the wizards. We failed. We found that the combinations were almost infinite, so we limited ourselves to a small subset of combinations that seemed to work well for us at the time. We documented these combinations in our team's Rules and Guidelines document (see Chapter 7). Over time, as we learned more about APEX and as new APEX versions became available, the combinations that we used evolved and improved. This evolutionary process illustrates a healthy application of Agile's principles of "*Continuous attention to technical excellence and good design*" and "*Regular adaptation to changing circumstances.*"

The following sections describe, at a high level, many of the core APEX components that are created by the wizards. The purpose of these sections is to show you the many options that are available to you when you use the core APEX functionality. The detailed usage of these options is well documented elsewhere in a number of Apress books.

Pages

Web pages are the fundamental building blocks of an APEX application. They are containers that hold regions, buttons, items, business logic, and navigation links. Components that are shared by many pages are also visible; examples are tabs, lists of values, breadcrumbs, and lists.

The page creation wizard is actually a grouping of related wizards that create a rich variety of pages that satisfy most business requirements. The APEX 4.x page wizards are as follows:

- Blank Page

- Multiple Blank Pages

- Report

  - Interactive Report

  - Classic Report

  - Report on Web Service Result

  - Wizard Report

- Form

  - Form on a Procedure

  - Form on a Table or View

  - Form on a Table with Report

  - Master Detail Form

  - Tabular Form

  - Form on a SQL Query

  - Summary Page

  - Form on Web Service

  - Form and Report on Web Service

- Plug-Ins

  - Items

  - Regions

  - Dynamic Actions

  - Page Processes

  - Authentication Schemes

  - Authorization Schemes

- Chart

- Flash Chart
- HTML Chart
- Map
  - United States of America
  - World and Continent Maps
  - Europe
  - North America
  - South America
  - Asia
  - Africa
  - Oceania
  - Custom Maps
- Tree
- Calendar
  - Easy Calendar
  - SQL Calendar
- Wizard
- Data Loading
- Feedback Page
- Login Page
- Access Control

The purpose of the foregoing list is to show you how much choice you have when creating web pages using only the core of APEX. The wizards create the pages together with the appropriate regions, items, buttons, tabs, breadcrumbs, DML processes, and validations.

Launching the Create Page Wizard is simple and fast (see Figure 3-2). The individual wizard steps are broken down into individual bite-sized pages that each contain a small number of related items (see Figure 3-3). In this case, there are eight individual wizard pages that are listed on the left. Stepping through the wizard is quick, simple, and accurate.

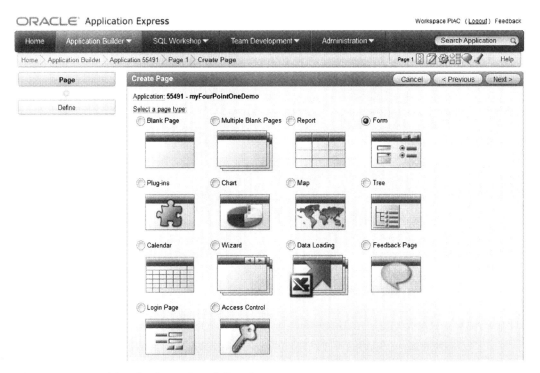

Figure 3-2. Launching the Create Page Wizard

Figure 3-3. Wizard steps to create a form on a table or view

Regions

Regions, like pages, are containers for other components. You create regions on pages where additional functionality is required that was not created automatically by the page creation wizards. APEX 4.0 introduced the concept of nested regions, a useful layout option. The region wizard options are summarized here:

- HTML
    - HTML
    - HTML Text (with shortcuts)
    - HTML Text (escape special characters)
- Multiple HTML
- Report
    - Interactive Report
    - Classic Report
    - Web Service Result
    - Wizard Report
- Form
    - Form on a Table or View
    - Tabular Form
    - Form on a Procedure
    - Form on a Table with Report
    - Form on a SQL Query
    - Display Only on Exiting Items
    - Master Detail Form
    - Form on Web Service
    - Form and Report on Web Service
- Plug-Ins
    - Items
    - Regions
    - Dynamic Actions
    - Page Processes
    - Authentication Schemes

- Authorization Schemes
- Chart
  - Flash Chart
  - HTML Chart
- Map
  - United States of America
  - World and Continent Maps
  - Europe
  - North America
  - South America
  - Asia
  - Africa
  - Oceania
  - Custom Maps
- Tree
- Calendar
  - Easy Calendar
  - SQL Calendar
- Breadcrumb
- PL/SQL Dynamic Content
- URL
- Region Display Selector
- Help Text

Mixing and matching pages and regions allows you to build web pages that contain a great deal of functionality. You probably noticed that there is a great deal of overlap between pages and regions. This is not surprising because very often the page wizards simply create a page together with an appropriate region. The region wizards allow you to add a mix of regions to a single page.

Buttons

Most buttons are created automatically by the page and region wizards. However, it is common to add buttons to a page to help with navigation or to launch business processes. The core APEX button creation wizard supplies two types of buttons:

- A button in a region position

- A button displayed among this region's items

The positioning of region buttons is controlled by a theme's templates. The positioning of buttons that are displayed among a region's items is controlled by the developer, who simply adds the button to a page in the same way as adding individual items like text boxes and select lists (see Figure 3-4). The fundamental difference between the two button types is found in their display properties. In this example, the Cancel button is displayed in the region template position that is defined by the #CLOSE# template substitution variable (see Figure 3-5). The Send Email button's position is defined by its sequence number and its HTML positioning properties Begin on New Line, Field, ColSpan, and Row Span (see Figure 3-6).

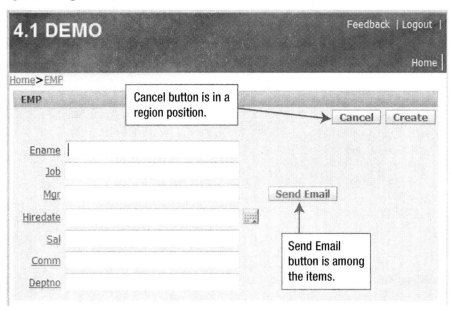

Figure 3-4. Buttons are in region positions or among the page items.

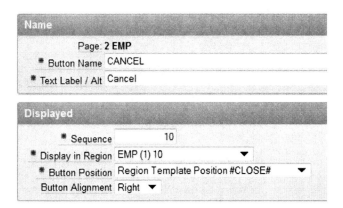

Figure 3-5. Display properties for a button in a region position

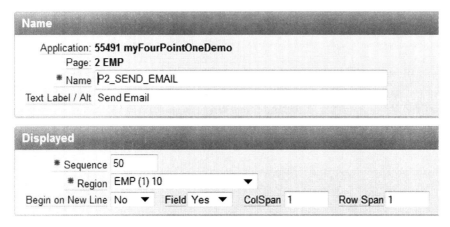

Figure 3-6. *Display properties for a button among the page items*

Items

APEX items are components that are equivalent to controls and widgets in other technologies. Core APEX gives you the following:

- Check Box
- Date Picker
- Display Image
- Display Only
- File Browse
- Hidden
- List Manager
- Number Field
- Password
- Plug-Ins
- Popup List of Values
  - Popup LOV
  - Color Picker
  - Text Field with Calculator Popup
- Radio
- Rich Text Editor

- Select List

- Shuttle

- Stop and Start Table

- Text Area

- Text Field with Auto Complete

- Text Field

Some of the items, like Text Field, are relatively simple and primitive. Others, like the Shuttle and Rich Text Editor, are sophisticated and clearly illustrate the fact that good-looking and good-quality applications can be built by using only the core APEX product.

The Shuttle is a composite of multiple HTML components that would be time-consuming to assemble by hand (see Figure 3-7). The Rich Text Editor consists of a significant amount of JavaScript that you do not have to write (see Figure 3-8). The declarative nature of core APEX makes these sophisticated widgets relatively quick and easy to build and maintain. The words "sophisticated" and "quick" are important adjectives that apply to both the core APEX product and Agile software development.

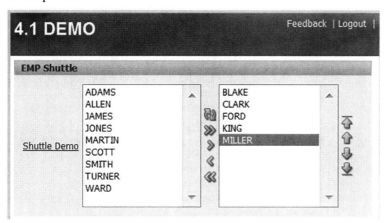

Figure 3-7. Shuttle item

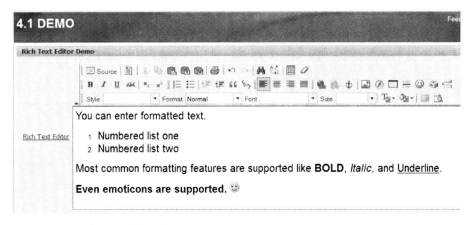

Figure 3-8. *Rich Text Editor item*

Computations

Computations are used to assign values to components on a page. The Create Wizard gives you three choices:

- Item on This Page

- Item on Another Page

- Application-Level Item

Computations are fired when a page is either rendered or submitted.

Computations that are associated with application-level items are powerful. Application items are, in effect, global variables in an APEX application. When they are used wisely, they can help an end user to juggle multiple contexts at one time. For example, a user could be doing some data entry on a customer record and then gets interrupted by a phone call from a second customer. By using computations on two application-level items, the user is allowed to easily switch back and forth between the two customer records.

Processes

Processes are used to run business code on a page. Like computations, processes are fired when a page is either rendered or submitted. Your options are as follows:

- PL/SQL

- Reset Pagination

- Plug-Ins

- Session State

    - Clear Cache for Applications (removes all session state for listed applications)

- Clear Cache for Current Application (removes all session state for current application)

- Clear Cache for Current Session (removes all state for current session)

- Clear Cache for Items (ITEM, ITEM, ITEM)

- Clear Cache for All Items on Pages (PageID, PageID, PageID)

- Reset Preferences (remove all preferences for current user)

- Set Preference to Value of Item (PreferenceName:ITEM)

- Set Preference to Value of Item If Item Is Not Null (PreferenceName:ITEM)

- Data Manipulation

  - Automated Row Fetch

  - Automatic Row Processing (DML)

- Web Services

- Form Pagination

- Send E-mail

- Close Popup Window

- Run On Demand Process

Some processes, like PL/SQL, are your windows into Oracle's database processing world. PL/SQL processes are used to call both your custom PL/SQL code and Oracle's incredibly rich set of database libraries. Your processing options are virtually unlimited. The simple example in Figure 3-9 could easily be running a few lines of PL/SQL code in the custom package or several million lines.

Other processes, like Session State and Data Manipulation, allow you to declaratively control the behavior of the APEX engine. The Session State processes are used to clear session state variables with a great degree of granularity. Data Manipulation processes declaratively encapsulate the code that creates, retrieves, updates, and deletes (CRUD) records in the database. The complex stuff, like record locking, is taken care of for you by the APEX engine.

APEX processes are an excellent example of Agile's principle of "*continuous attention to technical excellence and good design.*"

Figure 3-9. *PL/SQL process*

Dynamic Actions

Dynamic actions declaratively create JavaScript actions that control the behavior of items on a page. You choices are as follows:

- Standard

- Advanced

The standard wizard is a classic example of Agile's simplicity principle. It is designed to quickly install JavaScript code on a page that, for example, does simple things like enable or disable items based on common situations in which an item is null or equal to a certain value. The standard wizard is designed to do simple things fast. Figures 3-10, 3-11, and 3-12 illustrate how easy it is to disable several page items based on the value of a text item.

The Advanced Dynamic Action Wizard follows the same steps as the standard wizard. The main difference is the much richer set of triggering events that are available; for example, you can trigger the advanced dynamic action with events like Change, Click, Double Click, Key Down, Mouse Button Press, and many more. The standard Show, Hide, Enable, and Disable actions are augmented with advanced actions such as Clear, Refresh, Set Focus, Execute JavaScript Code, Execute PL/SQL code, and several others. Dynamic actions, which were added to APEX in version 4.0, eliminate much of the hand-coded JavaScript that was added in earlier versions of APEX and HTMLDB.

Figure 3-10. Creating a standard dynamic action: When page

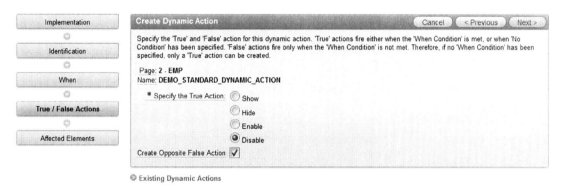

Figure 3-11. Creating a standard dynamic action: True / False Actions page

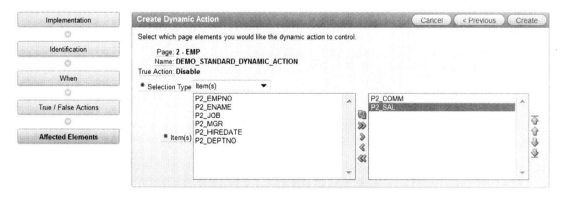

Figure 3-12. Creating a standard dynamic action: Affected Elements page

Validations

Validations do two things:

- They prevent bad data from getting into the database.

- They return meaningful messages to the end user.

APEX validations check for bad data when the user submits the page to the database. The validations fire in the database before the data is committed to the database. When an error is detected, control is returned to the user's browser, where a message is displayed. Ideally, the message should be phrased in terms that the end user can understand. The message should help the user correct the problem so that the user can carry on with his or her work. If the problem cannot be fixed by the end user, then he or she should be directed to use the Feedback mechanism that is part of the Team Development module (see Chapter 6).

Validations can be done on a granular item-by-item basis, in which individual page items are checked. Page validations are used when relationships between multiple items must be checked; making sure a start date is before an end date is a simple example.

The options are as follows:

- Page Item

    a. Not Null

    b. String Comparison

    c. Regular Expression

    d. SQL

        - Exists

        - NOT Exists

        - SQL Expression

    e. PL/SQL

        - PL/SQL Expression

        - PL/SQL Error

        - Function Returning Boolean

        - Function Returning Error Text

- Page

    - SQL

        - Exists

        - NOT Exists

        - SQL Expression

    - PL/SQL

- PL/SQL Expression
- PL/SQL Error
- Function Returning Boolean
- Function Returning Error Text

Branches

Branches control navigation to pages. They are often created automatically by the Create Page Wizards. You generally create your own branches when you add buttons and processes that must be linked to other pages.

Applications

The wizard that creates an application is incredibly powerful for creating the following:

- A starting point for a large application
- A complete simple application

In both cases, you step through a declarative process in which you choose what you want to create in the application. In APEX 4.1, the wizard's hierarchy is as follows:

- Application
  - Websheet
  - Database
    - From spreadsheet
      - Upload file, comma separated (*.csv) or tab delimited
      - Copy and paste
    - Instant application
    - As a copy of an existing application
    - From scratch
      - Based on existing application design model
      - From scratch
        - Add page
          - Blank
          - Report
          - Form
          - Report and form

- - Tabular form

  - Master detail

  - Chart

- Select tabs

  - No tabs

  - One-level tabs

  - Two-level tabs

- Shared components

  - Copy shared components from another application, yes or no

- Authentication scheme

  - Application Express

  - Database account

  - No authentication

- Theme

  - There are 23 themes to choose from in APEX 4.1.

  - Themes that are prefixed with an asterisk are IE 6–compatible (see Figure 3-13). This is handy for those of you still forced to support this archaic and difficult browser.

The main take-away here is that the Create Application Wizard makes it possible for you to build a small and simple application in literally a few minutes. Remember, to you the developer, a small, simple application may seem trivial; however, to the business user, it can be seen as a valuable resource if it solves a business problem and contributes to the bottom line.

For large applications, I recommend using the Create Application Wizard to build a minimal application with only a single home page. This seed application then quickly grows as you use the various component wizards to add the required functionality.

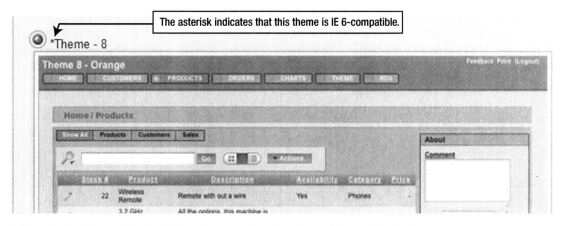

Figure 3-13. The Application Wizard gives a visual preview of the available themes.

Use Enhanced APEX

The term "enhanced APEX" refers to APEX applications that use supporting technologies to supply functionality that cannot be achieved by using core APEX alone.

Here are a few words of warning based on my experience. Most of us come to APEX after working with other products like Oracle Forms, .NET, Visual Basic, Delphi, etc. I came to APEX after ten or twelve productive years using Visual Basic. At first, I crafted APEX designs that were comfortable for me based on my Visual Basic background. The designs turned out to be awkward to implement in APEX, and eventually I stepped back and started to learn how to use APEX in the way it was meant to be used. Over time I learned how to do things the "APEX way." In the APEX world, plan "A" should always involve using the core APEX functionality where possible. This strategy is extremely Agile.

There are situations in which the core APEX functionality cannot meet your requirements and you must fall back on plan "B," which involves adding some supporting technologies to your APEX framework. Some reasons to use enhanced APEX are as follows:

- Branding requirements

- Training issues surrounding change management

- Specific functionality requirements

- Performance

- Reporting

Impact of Enhanced APEX

Stepping outside of the core APEX functionality has significant impact on many aspects of your development environment (see Figure 3-14). The obvious impacts are increased cost and extended schedule. Enhancing APEX means adding more moving parts in the form of added technologies. More moving parts means that your team must learn new skills by taking the appropriate training or by hiring new personnel who already have the skills. As the team size grows, you must move from lightweight project governance to a heavier-weight governance model in order to keep the team organized. Risk goes up as you add more moving parts; there are more points of failure, which increases the required testing effort and makes debugging problems harder. In other words, the more you enhance APEX with supporting technologies, the less Agile you become (see Figure 3-15).

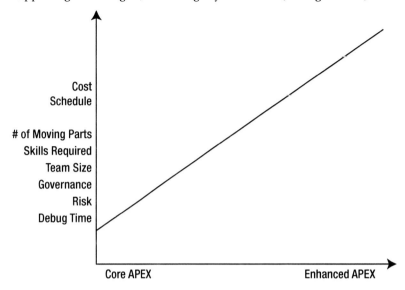

Figure 3-14. Effect of moving from core APEX to enhanced APEX

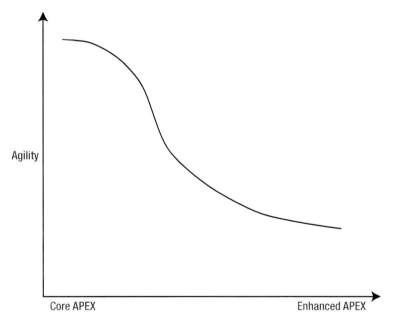

Figure 3-15. Enhanced APEX leads to less "Agility."

The foregoing paragraphs might lead you to believe that I am against using enhanced APEX. This is far from the truth. When you have a legitimate requirement that lends itself to using enhanced APEX, then use it; but use it wisely. You must make realistic estimates of the effect it will have on your cost, schedule, team, and customer.

It is also useful to note that using enhanced APEX does not mean that you are not Agile. You can apply Agile software development principles to enhanced APEX projects; in this case, you will find that your Agile governance model will have to become a bit heavier so that you can keep the project under control.

Business Cases for Enhanced APEX

There are probably a very large number of reasons for using enhanced APEX. I will speak to a few that I have come across over the last few years.

Branding

Organizations often brand themselves. The appearance of their web pages is extremely important to them. APEX utilizes a theme/template model that uses Hyper Text Markup Language (HTML) and Cascading Style Sheets (CSS). HTML is used to define the content of an APEX web page, while CSS controls how it looks.

The core APEX themes tend to be conservative and suit internal-facing applications extremely well (see Figure 3-16). Enhancing an existing theme or developing your own requires knowledge of HTML and CSS, together with a good understanding of how APEX builds its themes and templates. The results can be quite remarkable (see Figure 3-17).

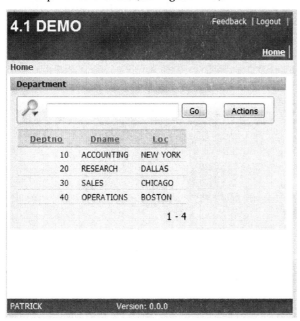

Figure 3-16. *Core APEX themes create conservative business GUIs.*

Figure 3-17. Enhanced APEX themes create branded GUIs.

Re-training

Many organizations have a long computing history that can date back to the 1950s or even a bit earlier. While I do not advocate building GUIs based on ancient dumb terminals, I do recognize the need to improve things without changing anything. This remark, of course, is facetious, but it does illustrate the crux of implementing change in an organization. Most people recognize the need for change, but they are comfortable with the status quo.

Years ago I was on a team that installed a new truck dispatch system in an open pit mine in Africa. The mine was replacing an older truck dispatch system that was not capable of moving forward. The mine personnel, being conservative in nature, were apprehensive about having to learn a new system. They relied heavily on a shift-end report for much of their daily work and communication. The mine manager, who was a very good people-person, asked us to duplicate the shift-end report precisely using the same header/footers, fonts, and layouts. The report did not fit our standard reporting infrastructure, so we coded it manually. The result was extremely positive; the mine personnel kept their shift-end report, which gave them a sense of continuity even though some other areas changed significantly.

The take-away here is simple. Enhance your template with a bright yellow "X" cancel button if that is what the users are using today; button design is merely cosmetic. Save your scarce training resources for the truly significant changes in the business processes.

GUI Functionality

Occasionally, users need something on a page that core APEX does not supply. In these cases, you can build the functionality by installing a JavaScript widget or an APEX plug-in (see Figure 3-18).

There are several open source JavaScript libraries available that contain handy widgets; two common ones are jQuery and Ext JS.

APEX plug-in technology is new as of version 4.0. Installing an existing plug-in into an APEX application is a relatively straightforward task. Creating an industrial-grade APEX plug-in is another matter; in fact, it is the subject of an entire book: *Expert Oracle Application Express Plugins* by Martin D'Souza (Apress, 2011).

Figure 3-18. Example of GUI functionality that core APEX does not supply

Performance

Core APEX performs most of its work on the server. Typically, a user makes a change on a browser web page and then submits it. The request goes to the server where the work is done, and the result is sent back to the browser. As the number of users and server requests increases, a point is reached where server performance is affected. The system architect has several choices to help make the application scale:

- Buy another CPU for the server

- Move some of the GUI work that is done on the server out to the browser via JavaScript

- Use AJAX to mitigate the amount of data on the page that must be refreshed

The capital and support costs of an Oracle CPU license must be weighed against the labor cost of coding the JavaScript and AJAX solution. This last point has been significantly mitigated with the introduction of dynamic actions in APEX 4.0. I expect that the need for hand-coded JavaScript and AJAX will diminish even further in future APEX versions.

Reporting

Core APEX does not have a built-in high-fidelity reporting engine. In this case, APEX developers are forced to look for solutions that are external to APEX.

The best technical choice is to use BI Publisher. BI Publisher works well with APEX and the learning curve is relatively shallow. Unfortunately, the capital cost is high and out of reach for many mid-sized organizations.

The alternatives to BI Publisher are several third-party reporting tools. Some are open source solutions; others charge a modest license fee. In all cases, the tools require more coding than BI Publisher; therefore, the cost trade-off boils down to capital cost vs. labor cost (see Figure 3-19). If you have a requirement for lots of reports and form letters, the labor cost involved in an open source solution will eventually exceed the capital and labor cost of BI Publisher.

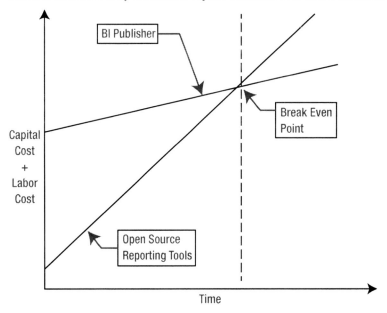

Figure 3-19. Capital and labor costs of BI Publisher vs. open source reporting tools

Wait for Future APEX Versions

Waiting for core APEX to eventually provide the enhanced functionality that you need can be a viable strategy, providing your customers have patience. This strategy entails an aggressive refactoring strategy when you upgrade your instance from one APEX version to the next.

Oracle's APEX development team has a good record of delivering new versions on an annual basis (see Table 3-1). Each new version that has been released contains significant improvements and enhancements, especially APEX 4.0, which contains dynamic actions and plug-ins. These two features have added a great deal of declarative browser-side control over the GUI.

The main risk that is associated with this strategy is that the enhancement that you need today might not be included in the next release of APEX. Mitigating this risk involves paying attention to Oracle's statements regarding the future direction of APEX. Another excellent source of information regarding the future of APEX is the Oracle APEX developers themselves. Many of them regularly attend the annual Oracle Open World (OOW) and Kscope conferences. The Kscope conference is organized by the Oracle Development Tools User Group (ODTUG). The Oracle APEX developers are regular presenters at the conferences and are happy to speak with developers after their presentations and at the networking functions.

Table 3-1. APEX History

Year	Version	Key New Features
2001	Flow Builder	Web development tool that was internal to Oracle
2003	HTMLDB 1.5	First release to the public
2004	HTMLDB 1.6	Themes, master-detail forms, page groups, page locking, multilingual capabilities
2005	HTMLDB 2.0	SQL Workshop, graphic query builder, database object browser, session state protection
2006	APEX 2.2	Packaged applications, APEX dictionary views, Access Control Wizard
2007	APEX 3.0	PDF printing with BI Publisher, migration tool from MS Access, page and region caching
2008	APEX 3.1	Interactive reports, runtime-only installation, improved security
2009	APEX 3.2	Migration helper for Oracle Forms, security enhancements
2010	APEX 4.0	Dynamic actions, improved charting engine, plug-ins, Team Development, websheets, RESTful web service support, enhanced interactive reports, improved Application Builder, better themes, APEX Listener
2011	APEX 4.1	Improved error handling, use of ROWID, data upload, enhanced calendar, easier-to-use websheets, improved validations in Tabular Forms, extended plug-in functionality, improved dynamic actions, optimized HTML, improved support for mobile frameworks

Use Another Technology

APEX is not the only web development tool in the world. There are many competing software development platforms that, like APEX, have strengths and weaknesses. There will be situations in which you will find that one of these competing platforms is better suited to the task at hand. Some of your options are as follows:

- *Oracle Forms:* If you have a large number of Oracle Forms applications in your shop, you might choose to stay with Oracle Forms and not bother converting to APEX or Oracle Application Development Framework (ADF). The risk here is succession planning; as your workforce ages, it will be hard to find young workers who are willing to use a development tool that appears static.

- *Open Source:* There are many open source products that can be used to build web-based applications.

- *.NET*: This tool is a popular development platform that is well supported by Microsoft.

- *Oracle Application Development Framework (ADF)*: Oracle is investing a lot in its Java-based Fusion technologies. ADF is a key building block in the Fusion technology stack.

Bear in mind that tool choice is determined by both technical needs and the cultural environment in which the technology is used.

Summary

The core APEX development environment is a software development platform that is ideally suited to lightweight Agile software development practices. This tool, in the hands of a skilled and motivated team, is capable of incredible commercial success.

There are situations in which you will need to use enhanced APEX functionality by adding external tools that complement the core APEX environment. Enhanced APEX, given the increased number of moving parts, will increase the cost of your projects and affect your entire software development environment. You will find that your team, while still adhering to the core values and principles of Agile, will need to embrace some of the "heavier" Agile practices in order to control your projects.

CHAPTER 4

Supporting Technologies

APEX can be viewed as a stand-alone web development tool, as a simple web development framework, and as a complex web development framework. The main difference between the viewpoints is the number of supporting technologies that are used in concert to achieve your desired results.

This chapter lists the technologies that support APEX together with some suggested tools (see Figure 4-1). The technologies are grouped as follows: classification

- Mandatory technologies required to make APEX work: without them, you cannot get started.

- Core technologies required in order for you to evolve from simple "hello world" applications to industrial-grade applications that are functional, robust, maintainable, scalable, and secure. The core technologies are associated with using APEX's "out of the box" strategy that emphasizes keeping APEX applications well within the boundaries of the APEX declarative environment. You will find that adding the core technologies to your development environment enables you to easily adhere to Agile's principle of "continuous attention to technical excellence and good design."

- Extended technologies used to build advanced web features that require expert APEX knowledge, or technologies that are outside of the APEX declarative environment. These technologies are added to an APEX application in response to advanced and sophisticated user requirements.

As you progressively add the mandatory, core, and extended technologies to your development environment, you should be aware that adding the technologies will:

- Slow delivery times

- Incur higher costs

- Require larger teams

- Add more complexity and risk

Happily, these issues can be managed effectively with an Agile approach. You just need to move a little bit from the lightweight side of the governance spectrum to a slightly heavier approach. Always remember to add supporting technologies and the required project governance to your environment by using the Goldilocks Principle: "Do not add too much technology, do not add too little technology, add just the right amount." Following this simple principle requires experience and good judgment. Since you are interested in Agile, I bet you have both attributes.

 Note Tool choice is extremely personal. Most programmers have strong and passionate opinions about their tools. The tools mentioned in this chapter are the ones that I and my colleagues use. There are many other excellent tools in the marketplace, so feel free to mix and match. However, teams that agree to use a common toolset are far more productive than teams that allow individual programmers to use the tools of their choice. Cooperative compromise in this area is an excellent application of Agile's fundamental principle of valuing individuals and interactions over process and tools.

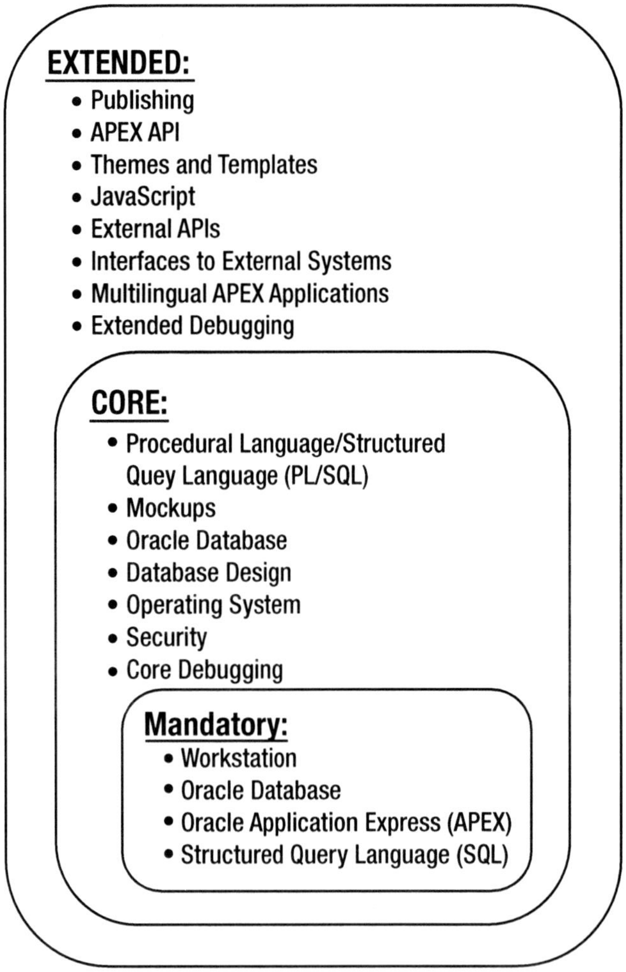

EXTENDED:
- Publishing
- APEX API
- Themes and Templates
- JavaScript
- External APIs
- Interfaces to External Systems
- Multilingual APEX Applications
- Extended Debugging

CORE:
- Procedural Language/Structured Quey Language (PL/SQL)
- Mockups
- Oracle Database
- Database Design
- Operating System
- Security
- Core Debugging

Mandatory:
- Workstation
- Oracle Database
- Oracle Application Express (APEX)
- Structured Query Language (SQL)

Figure 4-1. APEX technologies

Mandatory Technologies

Out of the box, APEX is simple; this, of course, directly supports Agile's principle of "simplicity." The basic setup requires only four things: a workstation, an Oracle database, APEX, and a rudimentary understanding of SQL. Table 4-1 summarizes these technologies and lists some of the common tools used to implement them.

Table 4-1. APEX Mandatory Technologies and Tools

Mandatory Technologies	Suggested Minimum Toolset
Workstation	Browser: Firefox Monitors: Minimum of two 21-inch monitors
Oracle database and a web server	SQL*Plus APEX SQL Workshop
Oracle Application Express (APEX)	APEX Application Builder APEX Administration
Structured Query Language (SQL)	APEX Application Builder APEX SQL Workshop

Workstation

Software developers spend a huge amount of time sitting at a workstation. The workstation is one of the most important tools in our development environment and one that is often overlooked as an important vector for productivity improvements.

A workstation is an ecosystem that consists of a desk, chair, mouse/trackball, keyboard, lighting, temperature, humidity, computer, reference books, noise, phone, printer, monitor, access to healthy food, access to water, office neighbors, and, in the center of it all, a programmer. Organizing this environment in a healthy way helps programmers to follow the Agile principle "sustainable development, able to maintain a constant pace." A workstation does not need to be pretty or expensive in order to be effective (see Figure 4-2). The main criterion is the provision of a comfortable and safe working environment.

Figure 4-2. *A comfortable workstation*

Ergonomics is out of scope for this book; however, I want to comment on one technical productivity tool that I think is important: large monitors. Large workstation monitors are, in my mind, one of the most important technical productivity tools in the web-based software development environment. A simple change to a web application often involves changing code in several files at once. Having two or more large monitors enables a programmer to display all the code snippets at one time so they can be viewed simultaneously. This strategy enables the programmer to see all the code snippets and, more important, their relationships. Case-sensitive variable names can be copied and pasted between applications to avoid subtle bugs. Using large monitors enhances productivity and assists programmers in their effort to follow the principle "continuous attention to technical excellence and good design." I single out large monitors because they are a relatively expensive part of a workstation setup compared to the other components, like keyboards and mice; some organizations see only the capital cost saving by buying small monitors without researching the ongoing cost due to lost productivity.

For APEX, the only mandatory workstation software is a web browser. You can develop APEX applications by using any of the common browsers on the market today; however, for serious development, I suggest Firefox. A number of plug-ins for Firefox, such as Firebug and the Web Developer toolbar, help you with HTML layouts and developing JavaScript code. There are other browsers, like Chrome, that can be equally effective. The browser landscape is evolving at a horrifically fast pace; it is hard to keep up.

■ **Note** A poor workstation environment can lead to nasty things like headaches, eye strain, depression, carpal tunnel syndrome, and ultimately rotten productivity. All of this can be avoided by taking the time to read and apply the tips and tricks found in a short article on office ergonomics. If a boss does not actively support this, then quit. No job and no amount of money are worth losing your physical or mental health.

Oracle Database

APEX lives inside an Oracle database; therefore the database is a mandatory tool. There are a number of ways that you can gain access to an Oracle database for APEX development:

- http://apex.oracle.com (free)

- Oracle Database 11g Express Edition (Oracle Database XE) (free)

- Oracle Standard or Enterprise Editions

- Cloud

Apex.oracle.com is a cloud-like free service that lets you sign up for an APEX workspace and schema. It is an ideal way for programmers to "kick the tires" of an APEX environment without investing any time in setup and configuration. The http://apex.oracle.com home page (see Figure 4-3) allows you to easily and quickly sign up for an APEX workspace in a few minutes. The page also contains a set of links that point you to the essential online APEX documentation; I highly recommend having a look at the Application Express Documentation and Oracle by Examples (OBE) links that are under the Getting Started heading. The only software tool you need in this environment is your browser. Note that you may not use this environment for production work; it is strictly used as a learning and demonstration tool.

Figure 4-3. *Apex.oracle.com home page*

The Oracle Database 11g Express Edition (Oracle Database XE) is a free, small-footprint Oracle database that you can download from

```
http://www.oracle.com/technetwork/database/express-edition/overview/index.html
```

Oracle Database XE is ideal for installing on a local workstation. The installation documentation is clear, so most developers have very little trouble getting the database up and running. APEX 4.0.2 is preinstalled and configured and requires no initial setup or configuration work. Upgrading to the most current version of APEX is relatively straightforward and only requires a rudimentary knowledge of SQL*Plus. The upgrade instructions that come with each download version of APEX are reasonably clear; however, the book *Oracle Application Express Recipes* (Apress, 2011) contains an explicit procedure that is a valuable help when used in conjunction with the upgrade procedure that comes with the downloaded version. This procedure is handy for developers who do not have an extensive DBA background because it is written for developers and explains the steps in detail without making assumptions about the reader's background.

Loading Oracle Database XE onto your local workstation is especially useful when you are building a custom theme. This strategy allows the template developer to develop and debug a new theme without impacting the rest of the team who are developing the application in a shared workspace. The new theme can easily be copied to the shared development environment and installed into the application that is under development after the new theme is thoroughly tested and debugged in the Oracle Database XE environment.

Many companies already have a licensed copy of an Oracle database. In this case, developers need to work with their DBAs to get the APEX environment set up and configured.

The cloud is now a reality. A number of commercial vendors will sell you access to an Oracle database. To use these services, you need to work with the cloud vendor to get your APEX environment set up and configured. Oracle, at Oracle Open World 2011, announced that it will make APEX itself available for production work in the cloud. Amazon offers an Oracle 11g database in its Amazon Elastic Compute Cloud (Amazon EC2) web service. This is a quick, easy, and cost-effective means of gaining access to a fully functional Oracle 11g database.

Oracle Application Express (APEX)

APEX is a mandatory tool. This is obvious. Good-quality, simple production applications can be built by using only the Application Builder and SQL Workshop modules. All of the absolutely essential aspects of application development are supported within the declarative APEX environment.

Structured Query Language (SQL)

You must have at least an introductory understanding of Structured Query Language (SQL) in order to build APEX applications. As an absolute minimum, you must know only one essential SQL statement:

```
SELECT * FROM MY_TABLE
```

This simple SELECT statement is all the code you need in order to build an interactive report. Of course, you will most likely need more than this as you extend your applications. Typically, for relatively simple applications, you can build your Oracle database declaratively by using SQL Workshop. SQL Workshop contains wizards that build tables (see Figure 4-4) and views and takes care of all the required INSERT and UPDATE SQL statements for you. In small and simple applications, most of your SQL coding work will be related to SELECT statements in reports, item defaults, and validations. The query builder (see Figure 4-5) that is built into the Create View Wizard is an excellent example of the fairly sophisticated graphic functionality that is built into the core APEX development platform.

Your skill with SQL must, of course, grow together with the size and complexity of your applications. SQL is a mature technology. Many books and courses will help you learn how to write efficient, accurate, and understandable SQL.

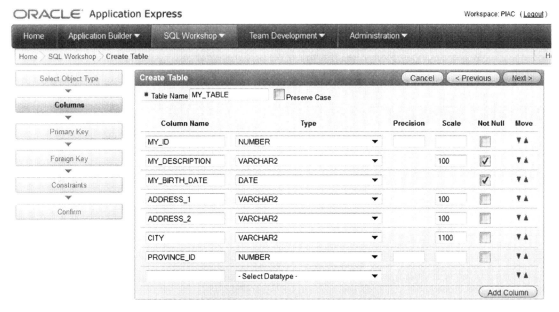

Figure 4-4. SQL Workshop Create Table Wizard

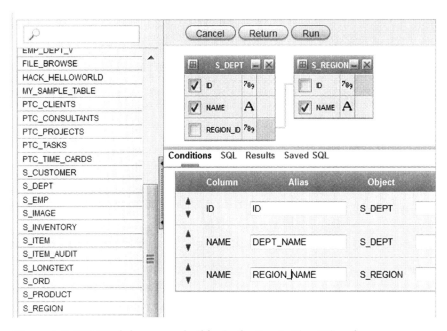

Figure 4-5. SQL Workshop query builder in the Create View Wizard

Core Technologies

The core technologies (see Table 4-2) are not absolutely necessary to build APEX applications; however, you will quickly find that they are required when you want to

- Improve your productivity

- Extend APEX functionality

- Write maintainable applications

- Build large applications

- Adhere to the core values and principles of Agile software development

Table 4-2. APEX Core Technologies and Tools

Core Technologies	Tools
Procedural Language/Structured Query Language (PL/SQL)	APEX SQL Workshop SQL Developer TOAD
Mockups	APEX Application Builder Wireframe and Mockup application
Oracle database	SQL Plus Oracle Enterprise Manager Oracle Application Programming Interface (API)
Database design	SQL Developer SQL Developer Data Modeler
Operating system	Text editor
Security	Lightweight Directory Access Protocol (LDAP) Oracle Single Sign-On (SSO)
Core debugging	APEX Debug APEX Advisor Firefox Developer toolbar add-in

Procedural Language/Structured Query Language (PL/SQL)

PL/SQL is the scripting language that is used by the Oracle database for manipulating data. APEX itself is a PL/SQL application; therefore it is not surprising to find that PL/SQL is one of the core technologies used with APEX.

PL/SQL is used to code business logic. It is a best practice to separate the GUI from the business logic. The separation of GUI and business logic is one of the first steps you take when applying the Agile principle "continuous attention to technical excellence and good design." In practice, you create one or more PL/SQL packages that contain procedures and functions that contain the business logic. Figure 4-6 shows you a snippet of PL/SQL code that is coded in the APEX Application Builder. The snippet contains business logic that might be handy in other areas, as well as some plumbing code. Figure 4-7 shows the same snippet after the logic and plumbing code have been moved to a PL/SQL package. The only logic left in the GUI is the call to the PL/SQL package plus the exception handling. Exception handling in the GUI is required because the GUI knows the context in which the end user is operating. Having easy access to the GUI components makes it relatively easy to give the end user an error message that makes sense to them and helps them to correct the problem so they can continue working without pestering the help desk.

All data items in the APEX GUI are strings. I have found it handy to push the data-type conversion work into overloaded routines that are paired with routines that do the real business work (see Figure 4-8). This removes plumbing clutter from GUI code. The routines that do the real business work are called with the expected data types—DATE, for example—so they can be called directly from other PL/SQL code without having to worry about redundant data-conversion work or depending on implicit data conversion.

```
Source
* Process  [Download Source]
DECLARE
   v_myDate    DATE ;
   v_myNumber  NUMBER ;
BEGIN
   :P0_ERROR_MESSAGE := NULL ;

   -- Convert APEX strings to the proper data types.
   v_myDate   := TO_DATE(:P1_MY_DATE, 'DD-MMM-YYYY') ;
   v_myNumber := TO_NUMBER(:P1_MY_NUMBER) ;

   -- Here are many lines of complex code.
   ...
   ...


EXCEPTION WHEN OTHERS THEN
   -- Log the error message here.
   ...
   -- Tell the user about the error
   -- and try to help them fix it.
   :P0_ERROR_MESSAGE := 'A helpful hint.' || ' - ' || SQLERRM ;
END ;
```

Figure 4-6. Anonymous PL/SQL block in the GUI with business logic

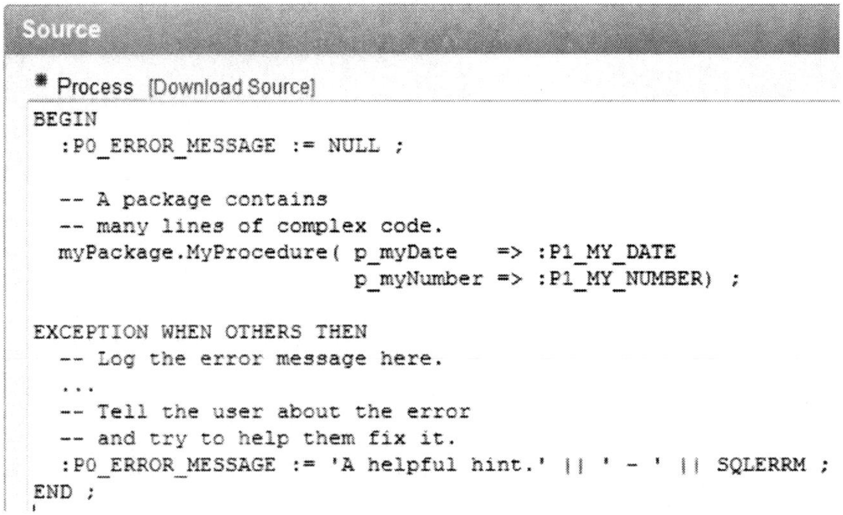

```
Source

 * Process  [Download Source]
BEGIN
  :P0_ERROR_MESSAGE := NULL ;

  -- A package contains
  -- many lines of complex code.
  myPackage.MyProcedure( p_myDate   => :P1_MY_DATE
                         p_myNumber => :P1_MY_NUMBER) ;

EXCEPTION WHEN OTHERS THEN
  -- Log the error message here.
  ...
  -- Tell the user about the error
  -- and try to help them fix it.
  :P0_ERROR_MESSAGE := 'A helpful hint.' || ' - ' || SQLERRM ;
END ;
```

Figure 4-7. Anonymous PL/SQL block in the GUI with business logic moved to a package

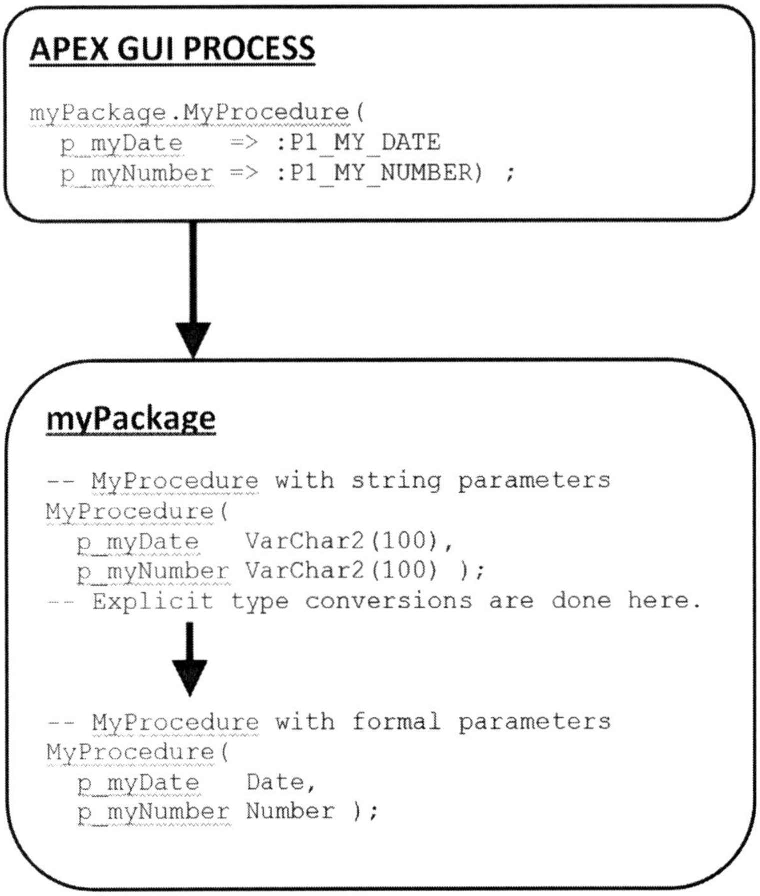

```
APEX GUI PROCESS

myPackage.MyProcedure(
  p_myDate   => :P1_MY_DATE
  p_myNumber => :P1_MY_NUMBER) ;
```

```
myPackage

-- MyProcedure with string parameters
MyProcedure(
  p_myDate   VarChar2(100),
  p_myNumber VarChar2(100) );
-- Explicit type conversions are done here.



-- MyProcedure with formal parameters
MyProcedure(
  p_myDate   Date,
  p_myNumber Number );
```

Figure 4-8. Use overloaded routines to eliminate data-type conversions in the GUI.

PL/SQL is a sophisticated and powerful procedural language. You thus need an industrial-strength tool for working with that language when doing serious development. The tool must

- Be convenient to use so you can code productively

- Be able to support effective unit testing outside the APEX context

- Have a good debugger so you can produce high-quality code

You have two tool choices from Oracle: SQL Workshop and SQL Developer. There are also third-party tool sets such as TOAD.

SQL Workshop, a module within APEX, is a quick-and-dirty PL/SQL development environment where you can code small and simple routines. It is not an industrial-grade PL/SQL development platform because the development windows in APEX 4.x contain no formatting or debugging functionality.

SQL Developer is a free Oracle tool that has recently evolved into a very effective PL/SQL development environment. It has many sophisticated features that support the full development life cycle.

Several high-quality licensed PL/SQL development tools are available in the commercial market place; TOAD is a good example.

Choosing the tool that is right for your team requires cooperation between developers. Most developers have their favorite tool set, but in a team environment it pays productivity dividends when the team members all use the same tool.

Mockup Tool

Mockups are useful artifacts to employ when you are beginning a software development project or adding a new module to an existing application. The act of building a mockup can be a wonderful design activity that is a delightful and productive collaboration between the software and business teams. Building a mockup collaboratively supports the Agile principle "Close, daily co-operation between business people and developers," and it is a great vehicle for facilitating knowledge transfer between the two teams.

APEX can be used as a mockup tool. The attractive advantage of this strategy is the fact that the resulting mockup is very close to a working prototype that can quickly evolve into the first version of the application; developers are attracted to this strategy because they are comfortable with the APEX development environment.

The disadvantages of using APEX as a mockup tool are as follows:

- Developing the mockup is a slower process.

- It's difficult for the business team to actively participate.

- The business team must have access to an APEX development environment.

These disadvantages combine to prevent the business team from taking active part in building the mockup. This point is driven home by Listing 4-1, which shows how you would mock up a simple APEX report; the business users probably would not be comfortable coding this on their own, especially when a large number of columns and rows are required to give a realistic picture of the proposed application.

Listing 4-1. Hard-Coded SQL Used to Mock Up an APEX Peport

```
SELECT      '345'           as ID
            05-MAY-1976     as Date_of_Birth
            'Doe'           as Last_Name
            'John'          as First_Name
FROM DUAL
UNION
SELECT      '346'           as ID
            12-SEP-1971     as Date_of_Birth
            'Doe'           as Last_Name
            'Jane'          as First_Name
FROM DUAL ;
```

A number of wireframe and mockup tools are available in the commercial marketplace. Some are free, and some cost a few dollars. Figure 4-9 shows a mockup of the report from Listing 4-1 together with several other easy-to-use objects that can be placed on the page with simple drag-and-drop technology. Many of the wireframe and mockup tools are file based, so little or no specialized configuration is required. Simple and intuitive interfaces enable both the development and business teams to quickly come up to speed with the tools.

The tool illustrated in Figure 4-9 is Balsamiq, an effective tool that costs less than $100. The Balsamiq mockup can be exported to a PDF file that contains active buttons and links. The active buttons and links allow the application designers to jump to the appropriate mockup page in the same fashion as the finished application; this type of mockup is extremely effective because the PDF file can easily be distributed to a wide audience via a shared drive or through e-mail.

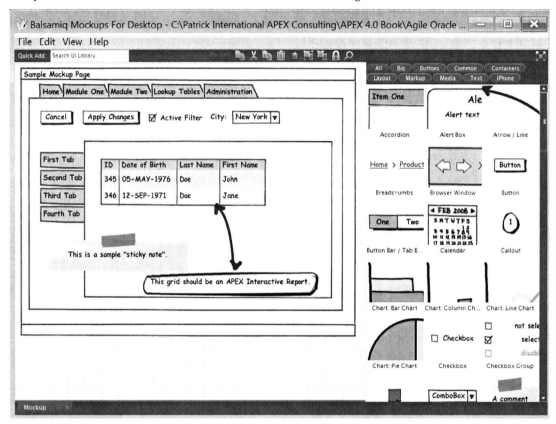

Figure 4-9. *A mockup is built using an easy drag-and-drop prototyping tool.*

Oracle Database

The Oracle Relational Database Management System (RDBMS) is huge and complex. Happily, APEX developers usually need only concern themselves with the data and programmatic aspects of the Oracle database and can leave most of the "under the hood" configuration and maintenance to professional database analysts (DBAs).

Some of the Oracle database data and programmatic objects that APEX developers typically use are

- Tables, indexes, views, and materialized views

- Foreign keys

- PL/SQL packages

- Code libraries

APEX developers can use SQL Workshop to build and maintain these database artifacts. However, as applications become bigger and more complex, it becomes more efficient to use industrial-grade tools like SQL Developer and TOAD. I personally use a combination of SQL Workshop and SQL Developer for my database development work; I tend to use SQL Workshop to create tables and views and SQL Developer for writing PL/SQL code.

The relationship with the Oracle database that contains APEX is straightforward (see Figure 4-10). The APEX engine is a large PL/SQL application that resides in an Oracle database. The APEX engine creates one or more workspaces that, in turn, contain one or more APEX applications. Each APEX application has a one-to-one relationship with a parsing schema that contains all the database objects the application needs to function.

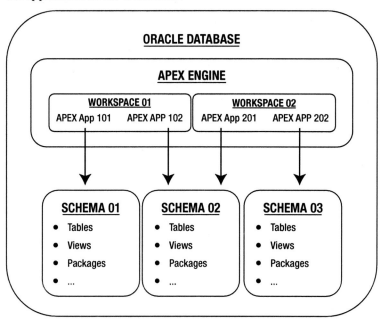

Figure 4-10. How APEX fits with the Oracle database

Database Design

APEX builds web interfaces on top of an Oracle database. A solid, well-crafted database design is critical to the success of an APEX application. As your APEX applications become more complex, you will need to use professional design tools like SQL Developer Data Modeler or one of its commercial counterparts like TOAD in order to

- Design the database

- Document the design

SQL Developer Data Modeler assists in the development of both the logical and physical designs of your database. The tool automatically generates the SQL statements that create the physical database objects. The tool contains a graphic interface that draws an entity relationship diagram (ERD) and enables you to print it on a large plotter (see Figure 4-11). The ERD is a valuable visual design tool that helps you to design complex data models. It usually evolves through several iterations before it is ready for construction.

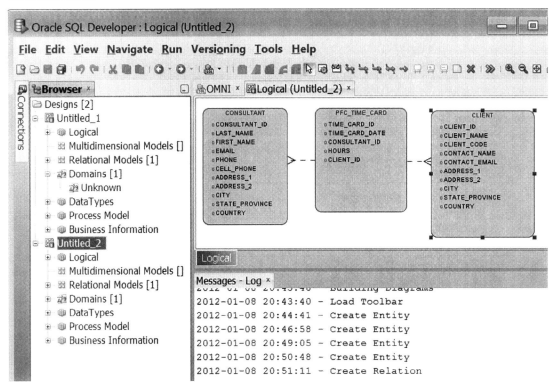

Figure 4-11. Oracle SQL Developer entity relationship diagram

Operating System Scripting

APEX usually runs on Windows or Linux servers. The developers who are in charge of promoting applications from the development environment through to the production environments need to become familiar with the operating system scripting tools in order to effectively automate the promotion process.

In general, a simple text editor is the only tool needed to build the operating system scripts. The traditional low-level text editors are notepad.exe for the Windows operating systems and vi for the Unix platforms. There are, however, a huge number of text editors on the market. Some tailor their automatic formatting to specific languages, and many contain language syntax checkers. Automatic formatting and color-coded syntax (see Figures 4-12 and 4-13) help programmers to code quickly and accurately by highlighting a program's structure and pointing out simple clerical coding mistakes.

A good working knowledge of the operating system command-line environment is also mandatory.

In addition, database tools like SQL Developer have sub-features that compare two database schemas. These are invaluable for ensuring that all the database changes, such as new columns and changed PL/SQL, are promoted from the development environment to the test and production environments.

```
Worksheet    Query Builder
 1  FUNCTION VALIDATE_PER_CENT( p_per_cent VARCHAR2) RETURN BOOLEAN AS
 2  -- Return TRUE  when p_per_cent is NULL or between 0 and 100.
 3  -- Return FALSE when p_per_cent is not numeric or out of per cent range.
 4  v_per_cent NUMBER ; v_return   BOOLEAN := true ; BEGIN
 5  IF NOT p_per_cent            IS NULL THEN
 6  -- If this statement fails, the exception will return false.
 7  v_per_cent                  := p_per_cent ;
 8  IF v_per_cent < 0 OR v_per_cent > 100 THEN
 9  v_return              := false ;
10  END IF ; END IF ; RETURN v_return ;
11  EXCEPTION
12  WHEN OTHERS THEN
13  RETURN false ;
14  END VALIDATE_PER_CENT ;
15
```

Figure 4-12. Raw, unformatted PL/SQL code

```
Worksheet    Query Builder
 1  FUNCTION VALIDATE_PER_CENT(
 2      p_per_cent VARCHAR2)
 3    RETURN BOOLEAN
 4  AS
 5    -- Return TRUE  when p_per_cent is NULL or between 0 and 100.
 6    -- Return FALSE when p_per_cent is not numeric or out of per cent range.
 7    v_per_cent NUMBER ;
 8    v_return   BOOLEAN := true ;
 9  BEGIN
10    IF NOT p_per_cent IS NULL THEN
11      -- If this statement fails, the exception will return false.
12      v_per_cent   := p_per_cent ;
13      IF v_per_cent < 0 OR v_per_cent > 100 THEN
14        v_return   := false ;
15      END IF ;
16    END IF ;
17    RETURN v_return ;
18  EXCEPTION
19  WHEN OTHERS THEN
20    RETURN false ;
21  END VALIDATE_PER_CENT ;
22
```

Figure 4-13. PL/SQL automatically formatted by SQL Developer

Security

Security in any computer environment is important. Security is divided into several areas:

- Authentication

- Authorization

- Session-state protection

The sections that follow go into each of these areas in a bit more detail.

Authentication

Authentication controls who is allowed to log on to an APEX application. APEX supports a number of authentication schemes:

- Application Express accounts

- Custom authentication schemes

- Database accounts

- HTTP header variables

- LDAP directory

- No authentication (using Database Access Descriptor [DAD])

- Open door credentials

- Oracle Application Server SSO

As you can see from this list, authentication schemes span a wide range from no authentication for purely public web sites to sites that are secured by integrating with an existing companywide operating system logon infrastructure using LDAP or Oracle SSO.

Authorization

Authorization controls a user's access to various parts of an application after the user logs on to your application. APEX is very granular in this respect: you can hide or disable large things like modules and pages as well as detailed artifacts like individual data items, buttons, and report columns. Authorization involves assigning roles to user groups and then writing a suite of PL/SQL boolean functions that are called from the APEX object you want to control.

Session-State Protection

Session-state protection is important for defending your APEX application from unauthorized hackers. Three common security vectors are

- URL tampering

- Cross-site scripting

- SQL injection

URL tampering occurs when hackers edit a browser's URL directly or edit hidden items on a web page. In APEX 3.2, the concept of session-state protection was introduced. Session-state protection adds a checksum to the URL that prevents hackers from manually changing a page number in a URL from an authorized page to an unauthorized page. This concept has become more granular in APEX 4.x (see Figure 4-14) by allowing more control options.

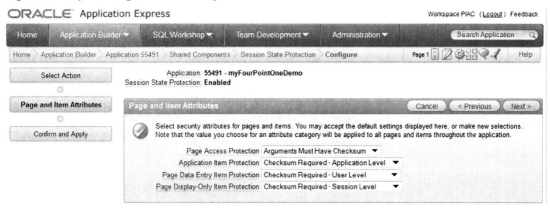

Figure 4-14. *Enabling granular session-state protection*

Cross-site scripting is done by injecting JavaScript into a web page. This can be done by entering malicious code into a comment item and saving it to the database. When the rogue comment data is returned from the database to the browser, the browser happily executes the JavaScript. The wizards in APEX 4.x now do a lot to protect programmers from this danger by automatically selecting items that "escape" data that is sent to the browser. For example, setting a report column to "Display as Text (escape special characters, does not save state)" explicitly stops JavaScript code in the column from being executed by the browser. The term *escape* refers to the process of stripping out JavaScript code from the data that is sent to the browser. It is still possible, however, for programmers to select item types that allow dangerous JavaScript to be inserted into a page.

SQL injection is similar to cross-site scripting. Instead of malicious JavaScript being injected into a web page, malicious SQL is sent to the database and then returns unauthorized data to the browser. In most areas of APEX, this is not a problem because the standard way of building SQL statements in APEX uses bind variables. Problems with SQL injection can arise when programmers build dynamic SQL statements when using the SQL report type "SQL Query (PL/SQL function body returning SQL Query)."

A detailed discussion of web security in an APEX environment is out of scope for this book; however, the book *Expert Oracle Application Express* (Apress, 2011) contains an excellent chapter on these topics and shows, in detail, how to prevent the problems in an APEX web environment.

Core Debugging Tools

Developers are not perfect. Sometimes you make mistakes, and then you have to spend time fixing them. These core debugging tools help you to fix mistakes:

- APEX debugging

- APEX Advisor

- Firefox Developer Toolbar add-in

The APEX Application Builder contains a built-in debugger that is useful for finding errors and performance issues in an APEX application. The APEX debugger is probably the first place you will look when you experience bad behavior in an APEX application. APEX debugging in APEX version 4.x must be explicitly turned on for each application (see Figure 4-15). Once debugging is turned on for your application, you can toggle it on for any individual page that appears to have a problem (see Figure 4-16). After you run a page with Debug toggled on, you can click the View Debug button to see the detailed execution plan for the page (see Figure 4-17), which lists every statement that is executed by the APEX engine as it renders your page. The time taken by each step is measured so you can easily see which statements are causing performance problems.

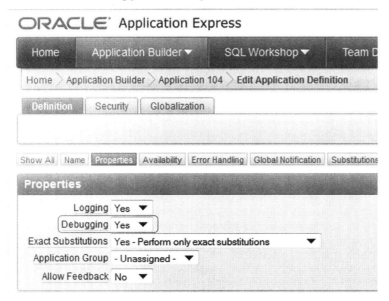

Figure 4-15. Turn debugging on in APEX Application Builder.

Figure 4-16. The Debug toggle is on each page.

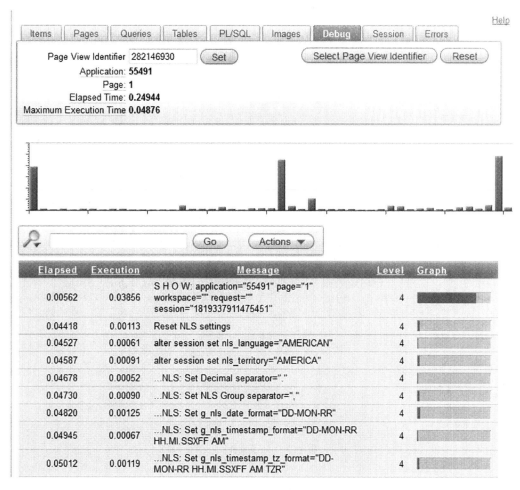

Figure 4-17. Debug shows precise times for loading a page.

APEX debugging exposes its API through the PL/SQL package APEX_DEBUG_MESSAGE. This package allows you to add log messages to PL/SQL code in APEX anonymous blocks and in any code that is called from within the context of an APEX application. The API is simple and effective. It consists of the following routines:

- ENABLE_DEBUG_MESSAGES

- DISABLE_DEBUG_MESSAGES

- REMOVE_SESSION_MESSAGES

- REMOVE_DEBUG_BY_APP

- REMOVE_DEBUG_BY_AGE

- REMOVE_DEBUG_BY_VIEW

- LOG_MESSAGE

- LOG_LONG_MESSAGE

- LOG_PAGE_SESSION_STATE

Expert Oracle Application Express fully documents this API and contains good pointers regarding its effective usage.

The APEX Advisor is a valuable tool for

- Finding bugs

- Areas where quality can be improved

- Areas where performance can be improved

Figure 4-18 shows the rich set of options available in the APEX Advisor. Hover over each check-box label to see a tool tip that give a little more information about the option. Figure 4-19 is an example of one line item from the APEX Advisor that gives you a flavor of the Advisor's style.

The Firefox Developer Toolbar add-in is a great tool for designing and debugging your web page layout. Figure 4-20 illustrates a simple web page whose table cells have been highlighted by the Developer Toolbar. You can imagine how helpful this tool can be when dealing with web layout issues. The Developer Toolbar does a lot more; it helps organize cookies, CSS, web forms, images, page outline, and many other page issues.

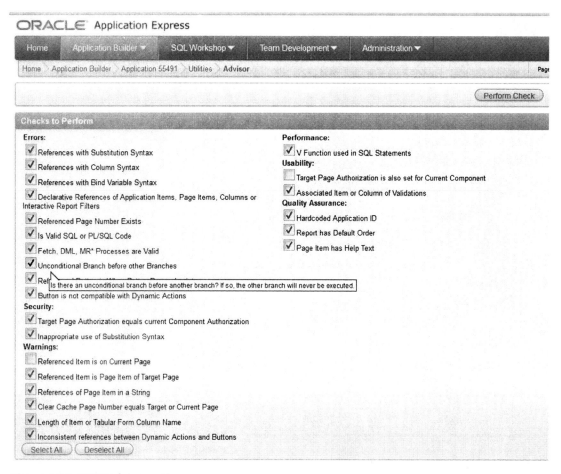

Figure 4-18. APEX Advisor options

Applications > 55491 - myFourPointOneDemo > Pages > 1 - Home > Regions > Department > Page Items > P1_FIRST_NAME	
Attribute	Item Default (When the item has no source or session state, use this default value)
Check	References of Page Item in a String
Category	Warning
Message	P1_LAST_NAME might not exist.

Value	BEGIN
	  return v('P1_LAST_NAME') ;
	END ;

Figure 4-19. APEX Advisor sample result.

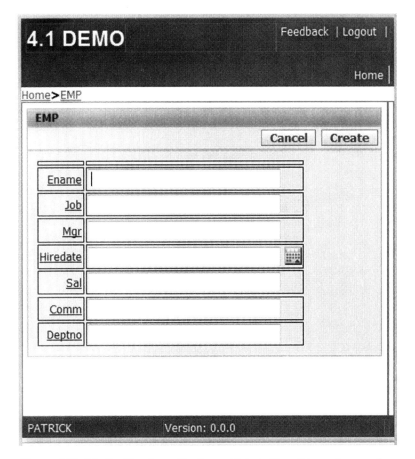

Figure 4-20. Firefox Developer Toolbar add-in table cell layout example

Extended Technologies

Table 4-3 summarizes some of the common extended technologies used in the APEX environment. The extended technologies and the suggested tools are used to add functionality that is not native to APEX. This list is not exhaustive; however, it gives you a good starting point for evaluating what tools and skills you need in order to extend and enhance the APEX framework.

Table 4-3. APEX Extended Technologies and Tools

Extended Technologies	Tools
Publishing	Oracle BI Publisher OC4J with Apache FOP XSL-FO processing engines PL/PDF
APEX API	PL/SQL
Themes and templates	APEX theme/template framework HTML CSS FTP tool (FileZilla)
JavaScript	JavaScript libraries DOM AJAX
External APIs	Google Yahoo!
Interfaces to external systems	Database links Web services
Multilingual APEX applications	APEX Application Builder XLIFF files
Advanced debugging	Firebug SQL Developer (remote debugging) Logger (instrumentation)

Publishing

Out of the box, APEX provides primitive printing functionality. Reports can easily be exported to comma-separated value (CSV) files that are printed using Microsoft Excel. Professional quality and well-formatted reports can only be produced by using one of the following external report engines:

- Oracle BI Publisher
- OC4J with Apache FOP
- XSL-FO processing engines
- PL/PDF

Oracle BI Publisher fits extremely well with APEX. One of its attractive features is the ability to format the report templates with an intuitive and easy-to-use plug-in for Microsoft Word. Unfortunately, it comes with a high license cost. The other options have inexpensive capital cost but require more coding effort.

APEX API

APEX has a rich PL/SQL and JavaScript API. These are used when the default Application Builder cannot meet a user requirement declaratively. For example, sometimes users want to see a multiselect list built using check boxes. In order to do this, you must loop through the lookup table and create a check box for each row in the lookup table. The APEX_ITEM package is used for this type of solution. The following is the list of APIs available in APEX 4.1. The names give you a hint about the kinds of procedures and functions that are available. The APEX home page documentation contains their detailed definitions:

- APEX_APPLICATION
- APEX_APPLICATION_INSTALL
- APEX_COLLECTION
- APEX_CSS
- APEX_CUSTOM_AUTH
- APEX_DEBUG_MESSAGE
- APEX_ERROR
- APEX_INSTANCE_ADMIN
- APEX_ITEM
- APEX_JAVASCRIPT
- APEX_LDAP
- APEX_MAIL
- APEX_PLSQL_JOB
- APEX_PLUGIN
- APEX_PLUGIN_UTIL
- APEX_UI_DEFAULT_UPDATE
- APEX_UTIL
- APEX_WEB_SERVICE
- JavaScript APIs

Themes and Templates

APEX 4.1 comes with 23 themes. These themes are used to build good-quality business applications and are largely interchangeable (see Figures 4-21 and 4-22). However, there are situations where the out-of-the-box themes must be replaced by a custom theme. Some companies have critical branding targets that require all public-facing venues, including web pages, to meet precisely defined graphic standards.

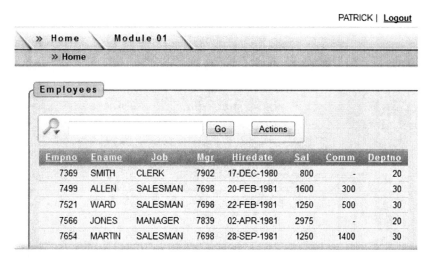

Figure 4-21. Employee report rendered by theme 10 - Sand

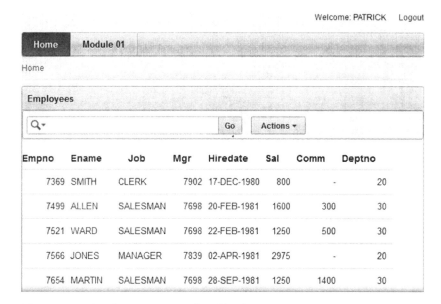

Figure 4-22. Employee report rendered by theme 23 - Crimson

In this case, the APEX development team must create a custom theme. Building a custom theme requires knowledge of

- APEX theme/template framework
- HTML

- CSS

- FTP tool (FileZilla)

Building an APEX theme and template framework is not yet a purely declarative process. You must dig into the existing templates and study how they are assembled. A good working knowledge of standards-based HTML and CSS is required for this work. You can test your HTML and CSS to make sure they conform to the latest standards by running your pages through the tests found at these sites:

- `http://validator.w3.org/`

- `http://jigsaw.w3.org/css-validator/`

APEX environments that use the Embedded PL/SQL Gateway store their CSS files in the database, not in the file system. You can access and maintain the CSS files by using a File Transfer Protocol (FTP) tool like FileZilla. Some web authoring tools like Adobe Dreamweaver enable you to edit the CSS files directly without having to go through the FTP cycle of download, edit, and upload every time a CSS change is required.

JavaScript

Prior to APEX 4.0, JavaScript was required if you needed to build an interface that competed with the rich user interfaces that are traditionally associated with compiled client/server applications using tools like Java, .NET, C++, and so on. With the introduction of Dynamic Actions in APEX 4.0, the requirement for JavaScript and AJAX has dropped dramatically. Dynamic Actions allow you to build JavaScript functionality declaratively, which eliminates a lot of hand-coded JavaScript and the related debugging headaches.

If you still feel the need to employ JavaScript, a number of JavaScript libraries contain many interface widgets that supply rich interface functionality. You must study these libraries carefully before using them in an APEX context. You also need to understand the web's Document Object Model in order to manipulate the page objects efficiently and effectively. A working knowledge of AJAX is also handy so you can do partial page refreshing to avoid full-page refreshes. Full-page refreshes can be painfully slow when you load your pages with the rich JavaScript UI widgets.

Public APIs

There are popular and well-documented public web APIs that can be used to add polish and pizzazz to your APEX web pages. Google Maps and Bing are good examples (see Figure 4-23). Integrating Google Maps into APEX applications is illustrated in a number of white papers presented at various Oracle conferences like Kscope, the annual conference hosted by the Oracle Development Tools User Group (ODTUG).

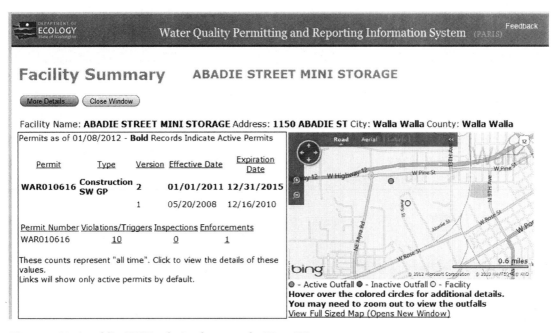

Figure 4-23. *A public APEX web site that uses the Bing API*

APEX Multilingual Applications

Both APEX and Oracle explicitly support multilingual applications. This is often a requirement in our multicultural and interconnected world.

The APEX application builder itself is available in a number of primary languages that are used in most of the developed world; an exact count is difficult as new ones are being added continually. English is the default language installed in a fresh instance of APEX. Scripts must be run after the initial English installation to translate the application builder into one of the other primary languages.

You build a multilingual application by first developing the application in one of the primary languages. The primary application is then translated to one or more of the 132 secondary languages supported by Oracle. Changes to the application are always done in the primary-language copy and then published to the secondary-language clones.

Publishing or translating an application from its primary language to a child language involves a number of steps. To get started, go to the Globalization menu in your primary application's Shared Components area (see Figure 4-24). When you select the Translate Application menu option, you are taken to the page that launches the utilities you need to translate your application (see Figure 4-25). Online help is available on this page. If you need a more detailed discussion of the topic, have a look at the book *Expert Oracle Application Express*, which contains a full chapter on this topic.

Figure 4-24. Globalization in Shared Components is the translation starting point.

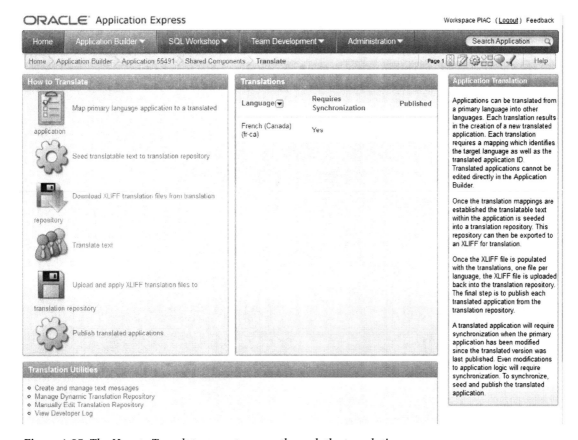

Figure 4-25. The How to Translate page steps you through the translation process.

Advanced Debugging Tools

Complex APEX applications need enhanced debugging tools that work in conjunction with the core debugging tools. The suggested toolset is

- Firebug
- SQL Developer (PL/SQL debugging)
- Logger (instrumentation)

Firebug is an add-in for Firefox. It enables developers to test and debug their JavaScript, HTML, and CSS work. The tool enables you to see the structure of your web pages side by side with the HTML and CSS code that generates the page. Firebug also enables you to single-step through your JavaScript code and inspect the values of the code's variables. It is a very powerful tool, indeed.

To launch Firebug in your Firefox browser, click the small icon in the upper-right corner (see Figure 4-26). This opens a world of debugging tools and options in your browser. Neatly formatted HTML and the related CSS are displayed immediately below your APEX application development area; this demonstrates the seriously practical power of Firebug (see Figure 4-27). You need to set aside a significant amount of time to learn how to use this tool effectively; however, it will be time well spent.

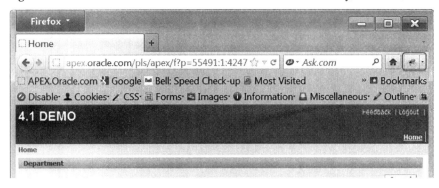

Figure 4-26. The Firebug icon launches Firebug in the Firefox browser.

Figure 4-27. Firebug in action

SQL Developer contains an easy-to-use PL/SQL debugger. To use this facility, you compile your PL/SQL package for debug and then click the bug icon (see Figure 4-28) to bring up the dialog that enables you to run a procedure or function in your package (see Figure 4-29). The PL/SQL block code is automatically generated by SQL Developer; all you need to do is change the values of the routine's input parameters. The PL/SQL block code can be saved and retrieved later, which is handy when many input parameters must be tested in multiple combinations.

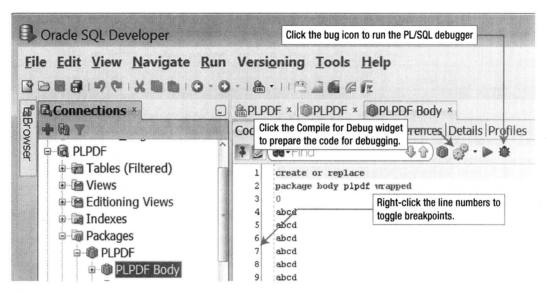

Figure 4-28. SQL Developer PL/SQL development page

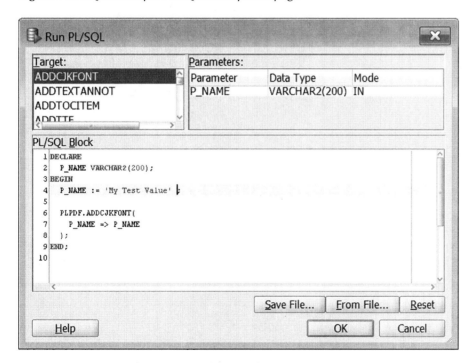

Figure 4-29. SQL Developer PL/SQL debugger launch page

Logger is a free utility that comes with excellent references. It is used to instrument your PL/SQL code and to log runtime errors. The code and its documentation can be downloaded from

```
http://tylermuth.wordpress.com/2009/11/03/logger-a-plsql-logging-and-debugging-utility/
```

Summary

APEX can be looked at as both a stand-alone web development tool and as a framework. APEX developers can produce good-quality applications by using nothing but APEX and a rudimentary knowledge of SQL. However, when you want to adhere to Agile's principle of "continuous attention to technical excellence and good design," you'll quickly find yourself adding core APEX technologies to your APEX toolbox. Adding polish and pizzazz requires going outside the APEX world to include things like JavaScript widgets and Google Maps.

Moving away from the basic APEX Application Builder requires more tools and skills. The larger number of tools and skills can be effectively managed within the values and principles of Agile software development; however, the governance effort must move from a lighter-weight model to a slightly heavier approach.

Project Management

Development and project management teams need one another; they have complementary roles to play in the game of building valuable software. Unfortunately, the relationship between developers and project managers can be somewhat uncomfortable; the amount of discomfort can range from mild irritation to outright hostility and mistrust. The discomfort is often caused by bad practices on both sides; developers often hide bad news, and project managers often pester developers with too many project management overhead tasks. Agile software development techniques help tremendously to mitigate some of these problems.

This chapter outlines the relationship between developers and project managers. Clearly defined roles, responsibilities, and accountabilities are necessary to make any relationship work. The roles are discussed in light of Agile software development in an APEX context. Next, we compare Agile software development with the traditional waterfall approach to project management. Developers need to be aware of the differences between Agile and the waterfall approach because many project managers have had many years of waterfall training and experience. Knowing the differences will help developers to communicate with their project managers more effectively. Finally, we will compare classical project management with Agile software development. Surprisingly, there is a good fit between classical project management and Agile software development. They complement each other nicely albeit with a bit of reshuffling of time lines and the addition of some Agile techniques that are specific to software development. As you read this chapter, keep the Agile value in mind that states "...*we have come to value responding to change over following a plan.*" And more importantly, remember that the item on the right, the plan, does have significant value.

Developer and Project Manager Roles

Developers dislike the overhead that is associated with project management; the project management overhead interferes with their primary purpose, developing software. Project managers dislike the absence and unreliability of time and status data; the missing or bad project management data prevents project managers from fulfilling their primary purpose, which is effectively managing the project and communicating with all of the stakeholders. This section looks at both perspectives.

Developer Perspective

As developers, our primary purpose in life is to develop high-quality and valuable software. This is our professional passion. The environment in which we develop software is usually a project environment. In a project environment, developers have secondary duties, which involve the following:

- Recording past time
- Reporting current status

- Estimating future time

Imagine being a Formula One race car driver. Your primary purpose and passion is to drive fast and win races. Exhilarating stuff. However, your environment consists of a car, race track, and pits where the car is serviced. Two or three times during a race, you must leave the race track and stop in the pits, where your crew changes all four of your tires, cleans your cooling air ducts, adjusts your front wings for more or less down force, and then sends you on your way. The pit stops are mandatory—without them you cannot finish the race, let alone win. The goal, therefore, is to minimize the time you spend in the pits so you can maximize the time you spend racing on the track. Formula One race car teams practice pit stops relentlessly so they are done effectively and efficiently. For example, a Formula One car is stationary in the pits for 2.9 seconds on a good pit stop; a bad pit stop is 3.4 seconds. We developers can learn a lot from the Formula One race car world.

The developer's secondary duties are like the pit stops in a Formula One race. The secondary duties pull the developer away from the primary activity of developing software; however, if they are not done and done well, there is high risk that the project will fail or be cancelled all together. Developers, therefore, must take the secondary duties seriously and organize them so that they are done well in a minimum amount of time. Similarly, management must play its part by taking care not to heap on so many secondary duties as to crowd out the primary.

Agile software development principles and techniques help to minimize the project overhead by emphasizing lightweight project governance. For example, the principles of "*face to face conversation is the best form of communication*" and "*close, daily co-operation between business people and developers*" encourage frequent verbal communication over formal written documentation. Of course, you must bear in mind that important decisions must be written down or they will be forgotten or misunderstood by some of the stakeholders. You must strike a balance between verbal and written communication and remember the Agile Manifesto's caveat that says "*...while there is value in the items on the right, we value the items on the left more.*" Written requirements and design documents have value; just remember to keep them as terse as possible, making them both short and effective.

APEX provides tools that are effective in minimizing project management overhead. The edit page in Application Builder is linked directly to the To Do page in Team Development (see Figure 5-1). The upper right corner of the page contains four links, three of which go directly to the Team Development To Do, Bug, and Feedback pages. Of special interest here is the link to the To Do page (see Figure 5-2), where a developer can quickly navigate to a To Do that is associated with the current page. The To Do landing page, in this case, contains an interactive report that is pre-filtered for the current application, the current page, and for a status that is less than 100% complete. One additional click takes the developer to the individual To Do page, where the To Do's status is updated and the estimated time is replaced with the actual time (see Figure 5-3). This activity should take well under 60 seconds. By taking your development "pit stops" seriously, you will keep your "pit stop" time to a minimum, which will give you more time for the fun stuff, like developing software.

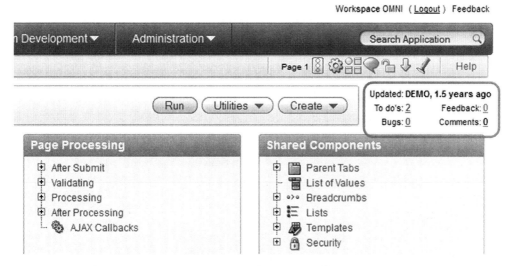

Figure 5-1. Links to Team Development in Application Builder

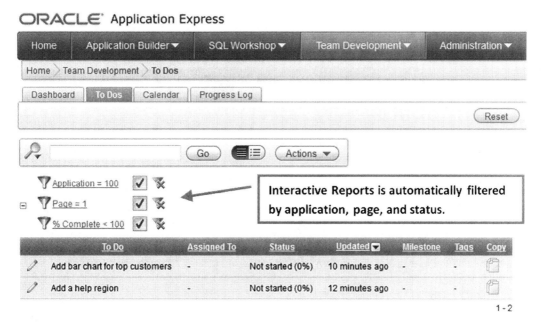

Figure 5-2. To Do landing page from Application Builder

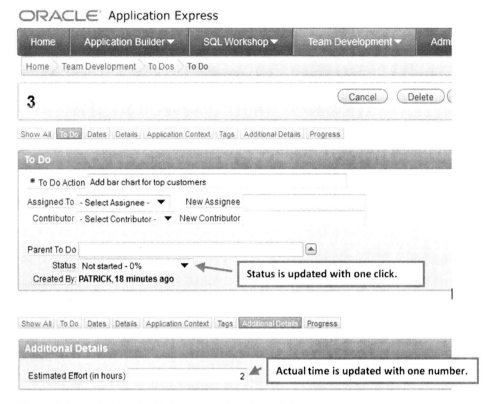

Figure 5-3. *Updating a To Do's status and estimated time*

Project Manager Perspective

Project managers, according to the Project Management Institute (PMI), spend a high proportion of their time communicating. They must orchestrate a project so that everyone's time is respected and used optimally. In order for them to perform effectively in a software development environment, they need accurate time recording, task status information, and good-quality time estimates from developers. Without these inputs, they are effectively blind, which makes them very uncomfortable indeed.

How can a project manager take advantage of Agile and APEX to encourage the developers to supply the needed data? The first step is the realization that moving from classical project management to Agile requires a major shift in attitude for the classical project manager. The one particular value in the Agile Manifesto that gives many classical project managers trouble is "...*we have come to value responding to change over following a plan.*" A plan is static—it is out of date before the ink on the paper is dry. It is important to remember that while the plan has value, the planning process has more value. This thought was captured by Dwight D. Eisenhower when he said, "*In preparing for battle I have always found that plans are useless, but planning is indispensable.*" The Agile technique of holding a daily stand-up meeting acts as an effective steering mechanism for a project. A plan is put into place and is adjusted every day in response to the previous day's accomplishments or failures. Kent Beck, one of the signatories of the Agile Manifesto and proponent of Extreme Programming, likens the daily stand-up meeting to driving a car. The car is pointed in a direction (the plan), and then, as the car moves forward, the driver constantly makes minor direction changes with the steering wheel (the planning process) to keep the car on the road. If you don't steer, you eventually drive off the road.

An important artifact in a project plan is the work breakdown structure (WBS). In a classical project management environment, the WBS is fully fleshed out in great detail before work begins. The WBS is used to both estimate the cost and schedule of a project and to control the project as it unfolds. The failure of this approach in the software world is one of the reasons that Agile was born.

The Agile approach to building a WBS is to keep the WBS at a high level and flesh out the details only when the work on an iteration begins. Project managers must avoid micro-managing their developers. Micro-managing flies in the face of the Agile principle *"projects are built around motivated individuals, who should be trusted."*

APEX's Team Development module is a good tool for organizing a project's high-level Features and To Dos (tasks). Each team must decide how much or how little detail to capture in Team Development. Several rules of thumb will be needed to define what is captured formally in Team Development. For example, create a To Do for tasks that do the following:

- Take more than four hours to complete

- Affect one or more other To Dos—in other words, tasks that have dependencies

A detailed WBS is necessary to complete a line item in the To Do list. The detailed WBS can reside in a developer's head or be written on a scrap of paper (see Figure 5-4). There is no need to spend the time capturing micro-details in the formal electronic WBS, as the micro-historical data is generally worthless. The value of the micro-WBS resides in the immediate process of getting the work done. Personally I prefer a micro-WBS that is written on a scrap of paper over the "in the head" WBS. Writing the WBS down forces the developer to think through all of the steps; often an obscure step is identified that would be otherwise missed. Missing snippets of code are very difficult to find and fix, especially when a second developer inherits the code; mind reading is difficult, especially when one of the minds is no longer available. Another valuable benefit to an informal, written WBS is that you can pick up where you left off when you are interrupted.

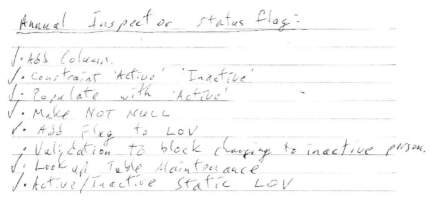

Figure 5-4. Programmer's personal work breakdown structure (WBS) for a small task

A developer trait that is valuable to project managers is honesty. Project managers must encourage and promote honest communication with developers. Agile's promotion of the daily stand-up meeting is one of the best ways to encourage this honesty. In this forum, problems are exposed early. When problems are exposed early, then there is more time available to address and fix them. Failing early in a project is always better than failing late in a project.

Agile vs. Waterfall

Agile software development was born in a rebellion against waterfall project management. Waterfall project management is one of the reasons for the software industry's horrible record of project failures. Failure is defined as projects being significantly late, overbudget, poor quality, or cancelled.

In a nutshell, waterfall software development refers to carrying out the following processes sequentially (see Figure 5-5):

- Gather requirements

- Design

- Build

- Test and debug

- Implement

Each phase is completed before moving on to the next phase. Detailed reviews are conducted before the stakeholders sign the phase completion documents. The model is simple and understandable.

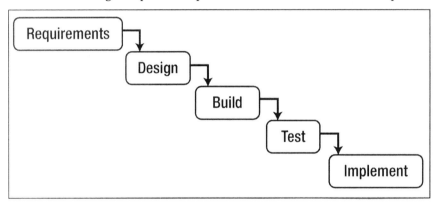

Figure 5-5. Waterfall project management

In theory, rigorous planning at the beginning of a project finds most requirement and design bugs before construction begins. Bugs are easier and cheaper to fix in the planning stage when compared to finding and fixing the same bug after construction begins. Waterfall software is heavy in the documentation area. Thick documents capture the requirements and design and have value when the project's personnel changes.

In practice, waterfall project management works well in some industries like construction; however, in the software industry, it has failed. There are several reasons for this failure. The software industry is new and is not yet fully mature when compared to industries like construction, which has thousands of years of experience. Our hardware and software platforms change dramatically every year, whereas most other industries measure change in decades and even centuries; the art of bricklaying has not changed much in over a hundred years. Our users' expectations constantly move our goalposts with regards to quality. In short, heavy upfront planning in this dynamic environment is risky; a two-year detailed IT plan is doomed within six months. Agile recognizes this situation and plans for it by keeping the upfront planning at a high level and leaving the detailed planning to individual, small iterations that occur as the project unfolds. Taking a lesson from the manufacturing industry, we can think of this as "just in time planning."

Agile software development is now being officially supported by the Project Management Institute (PMI). In 2011, PMI added an Agile certification to its suite of professional credentials. The "PMI Agile Certified Practitioner (PMI-ACP)" now stands beside PMI's most well-known credential, the "Project Management Professional (PMP)." PMI's online bookstore and suite of project management white papers are now filled with books and articles dealing with Agile software development. Agile is now mainstream.

Agile Complements Traditional Project Management

The Project Management Institute (PMI) was formed by an altruistic group of project professionals who recognized that there is a great deal of commonality in how all industries manage projects. PMI was born in the 1970s and is now one of the world's largest international professional membership organizations. Its membership has passed the half-million mark, with active chapters in more than 185 countries. PMI is responsible for one of the world's most common and sought-after project management credentials, the Project Management Professional (PMP). PMI maintains and publishes *A Guide to the Project Management Body of Knowledge (PMBOK Guide)*; this guide is one of the main texts studied by certified project managers. PMI is the bastion of traditional project management theory, practice, and techniques.

If you are a software developer in a medium- to a large-size organization, chances are that one or more of your project managers have earned their PMP designation. This chapter steps through the key aspects of traditional project management and shows how Agile complements traditional project management. This material will help you communicate effectively with your project managers.

The *PMBOK Guide* is organized around five project management process groups.

- Initiating

- Planning

- Executing

- Monitoring and Controlling

- Closing

There are nine knowledge areas that relate to the process groups.

- Integration Management

- Scope Management

- Time Management

- Cost Management

- Quality Management

- Human Resources Management

- Communication Management

- Risk Management

- Procurement Management

As an experienced and skilled software developer, you will probably recognize and relate to all of the process groups and knowledge areas. The headings are intuitive.

The only process group that touches all of the knowledge areas is the planning process. This fact probably accounts for why traditional project managers put so much time and effort into planning. Planning accounts for a large proportion of their training.

The matrix of project management process groups and knowledge areas consists of 26 areas that contain specific outputs and activities.

- Initiating
  - Integration Management
  - Communication Management
- Planning
  - Integration Management
  - Scope Management
  - Time Management
  - Cost Management
  - Quality Management
  - Human Resources Management
  - Communication Management
  - Risk Management
  - Procurement Management
- Executing
  - Integration Management
  - Quality Management
  - Human Resources Management
  - Communication Management
  - Procurement Management
- Monitoring and Controlling
  - Integration Management
  - Scope Management
  - Time Management
  - Cost Management
  - Quality Management
  - Communication Management

- Risk Management
- Procurement Management
- Closing
  - Integration Management
  - Procurement Management

Both Agile and traditional project management deal with all process groups and knowledge areas. The main difference between traditional project management and Agile is in the timing. Traditional project management tends to organize projects in a waterfall-like manner, in which the requirement gathering and design are done in great detail before the executing process begins. Does traditional project management dictate that waterfall be used exclusively? No. Traditional project management actually recognizes that there is significant overlap between the five process groups. Figure 5-6 illustrates what the five process groups look like when they are executed sequentially. The only process group that spans the entire project is Monitoring and Control. Strict waterfall project management rarely occurs because the requirements and design must be adjusted to account for bugs, omissions, and minor changes in the requirements and design. Figure 5-7 illustrates the level of interaction between the process groups over time from the perspective of PMI's traditional view of project management. Often, this time-based view is based on project phases that generally have longer time scales than Agile's short and time-bound iterations.

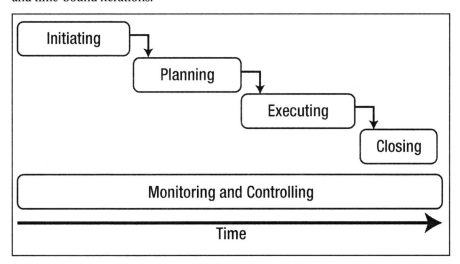

Figure 5-6. Waterfall view of project process interaction

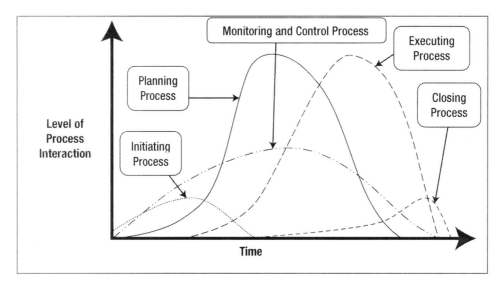

Figure 5-7. *Traditional project management view of project process interaction*

Agile builds on traditional project management by acknowledging the existence of all of the traditional process groups. Figure 5-8 illustrates how Agile deals with the timing of project management by subdividing the overall (macro) project plan into iterations (micro) project plans. The overall initiation and planning processes are done at a high level. The planning and estimates are fleshed out only to the point where budgetary figures for cost and schedule are deemed reliable enough to get permission to begin the project. Note that you can produce reliable budgetary figures accurately without being overly precise.

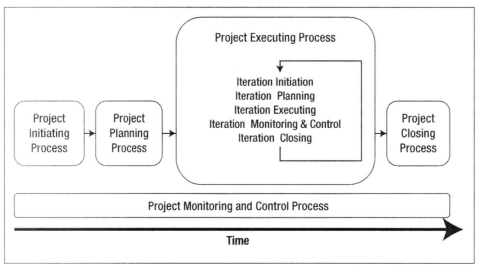

Figure 5-8. *Agile view of project process interaction*

Planning poker is a methodology that is useful in the area of estimating budgetary time for both overall project estimates and individual iteration estimates. Planning poker is sometimes called scrum poker, which acknowledges its birthplace. Planning poker gives each person in a group of experienced software professionals a deck of cards that contains a Fibonacci sequence, one number per card. The sequence is 0, 1, 2, 3, 5, 8, 13, 21, 34, 55, and 89. Note that you could easily substitute any set of relative terms for the Fibonacci sequence; small, medium, large, and extra-large can be used just as effectively. The game is played by selecting a software feature or a task and having each player put down a card that represents his or her estimate of the relative effort required to complete the feature or task. If everyone plays the same card, the number is recorded and the team moves on to the next feature. If different cards are played then the team members discuss why they picked their number. Discussion continues until a consensus is reached. After the relative values of effort for each feature or task have been established, then time values are assigned to the relative numbers so that the schedule can be estimated. A Fibonacci two could be two hours, two days, two weeks, or two months, depending on the planning scale.

Agile Mapping to Traditional Project Management

This section steps through the traditional project management process groups and knowledge areas to illustrate how APEX and Agile fit into the traditional view of project management. Understanding this mapping helps us software developers to communicate with our project managers and helps us understand what is required of us from a project management perspective, so that we can minimize our project management overhead without compromising the project management quality.

Initiating

The start of a project or an iteration requires a kick-off. The initiating process covers both.

Integration Management: Initiating

Traditional project management calls for a project charter to be written to initiate the project. The project charter's main purpose is to define the project's scope, costs, schedule, and probability of success to a point where higher management can feel comfortable giving permission to begin the project.

A developer's input to the project charter is generally confined to the technical viability of the riskier requirements and estimating the high-level amount of effort that is required to construct the application's features.

The beginning of an iteration is much different. Developers are intimately involved with all aspects of an iteration. Developers work closely with the business team to hammer out the requirements. The number of features that are included in an iteration is dictated by the development team's time estimates.

Communication Management: Initiating

Project managers are responsible for identifying all of the stakeholders at the beginning of a project. Once the stakeholders are identified, your role as a developer is to reach out to the stakeholders with whom you will be working. The two main teams that need to be contacted are the business and testing teams. A face-to-face kick-off meeting is an ideal venue, where everyone meets and shakes hands. This is the "forming" stage of the "forming, storming, norming, performing" group development model (as

described by Bruce Tuckman in 1965—see
`http://en.wikipedia.org/wiki/Tuckman's_stages_of_group_development`).

Planning

The planning process group touches all nine project management knowledge areas.

Integration Management: Planning

The main output of integration management in the high-level planning process is the project management plan. One of the Agile methodologies is selected or a home-grown methodology is defined.

Scope Management: Planning

Part of the high-level planning process is scope refinement. The project charter already contains a high-level scope; however, it might need further technical work related to dependencies before individual features can be sequenced.

Scope management at the beginning of an iteration consists of picking a small number of features and tasks that can be reliably completed in the iteration's allotted time.

Time Management: Planning

Time management in the software industry is one of the most important aspects of project planning, both at the overall level and at the iteration level. Time in our world equates to money.

The outputs of time management at both the overall and iteration scales are as follows:

- Sequence of activities

- Resource estimates

- Activity duration

- Schedule

The overall sequence of activities should be ordered so that high-value features are delivered to the customer first. When the overall project is managed this way, the customer will have received valuable working software even if the project is cancelled before its scheduled finish. In an iteration, the sequence is often governed only by the technical dependencies.

The sequence in which features are delivered dictates when resources are scheduled to work on the project. Some resources—DBAs, for example—are not full-time team members; they parachute into the project for short stints and then leave.

Duration estimating is vitally important for both the overall project and individual iterations. Duration drives the schedule.

Building the project schedule involves translating time durations into calendar dates. Each feature and task is matched to an available resource, and the time duration is converted to calendar duration by accounting for the availability of the resource, the amount of time that the resource has available for the project work, and the pace at which the resource works; a senior resource will have a faster pace than a junior resource.

Cost Management: Planning

Cost management is usually owned by the project manager, the accounting team, or higher-level management. Developers normally deal with cost indirectly by using time as their currency.

Quality Management: Planning

Quality management at the overall planning stage is often spoken of in terms of performance requirements, online help availability, and ease-of-use. Developers, based on the high-level requirements, tell the other teams what is technically achievable. For example, the developers might say that most queries will run in under one second except for a few that will take five seconds. If the business users demand that the five-second queries be reduced to one second, then the developers must articulate if the one-second target can be hit and, if so, what impact it will have on cost and schedule.

Quality management at the iteration level is a developer's sweet spot. There is a huge amount of passion involved here when a highly motivated and skilled team of developers is involved. Agile's principle of "continuous attention to technical excellence and good design" comes to the fore in this area when the team plans for quality by formulating a rules and guidelines document (see Chapter 7).

Human Resource Management: Planning

Many organizations manage human resources from the top down. Management identifies the roles, responsibilities, skill sets, and reporting relationships that are required by the project; then they assign people to the roles.

Agile works with a bottom-up philosophy that is based on the Agile principles of "*projects are built around motivated individuals, who should be trusted*" and "*self-organizing teams.*" At the beginning of a project, many of the team members are new to each other and unsure of the roles they will play; therefore, they will go through the "storming" part of the "forming, storming, norming, performing" team development model. The "storming" quickly moves on to the "norming" when the individual team members possess a good level of emotional maturity. In my opinion, Agile requires a high level of emotional maturity to be successful. This is an area where a skilled project manager adds a great deal of value by mentoring team members who need help in this critical soft-skill area.

Communication Management: Planning

Traditional project management calls for setting up a communication plan. Information must flow from the shop floor up to high-level management and stakeholders. This plan must be in place for both traditional and Agile project environments. APEX offers several tools and techniques that can automate much of the communication overhead (see Chapter 8).

In an Agile environment, the working environment is generally much different from the traditional setup. First, individual office cubes are replaced with an open office environment that has no walls. Privacy is respected by setting up a closed-door area where team members can make their private phone calls and write private e-mails. Second, the development, business, and testing teams set up their workstations to be as close as possible physically. If physical co-location is not possible, then remote communication technologies must be set up so that conference calls and screen sharing sessions are quick and easy to organize on short notice. Co-location and remote communication technology directly support Agile's principles of "*close, daily co-operation between business people and developers*" and "*face-to-face conversation is the best form of communication.*" Working in a big, open room might sound like a recipe for disaster where everyone is constantly being interrupted either directly or indirectly by background chatter. There are several Agile techniques that mitigate the potential open office chaos. The daily stand-up meeting is used to communicate many of the routine status updates. The team can agree to a scheduled "heads-down" time, when phones and e-mails are turned off and conversation is kept to a minimum. Team members who need to discuss an issue can move to a closed-door boardroom so as not to disturb their teammates. On a lighter note, I worked in an open environment with a PhD mathematician who was tasked with coding very tricky three-dimensional underground views of an underground mining property. He donned a pair of bright orange industrial ear protectors when he needed some serious heads-down time. Everyone respected him and his time.

Risk Management: Planning

Risk planning involves looking into a crystal ball to predict what can go wrong with a project and what positive opportunities might present themselves. PMI's *PMBOK Guide* devotes an entire chapter to risk management that outlines a formal and heavyweight approach to risk planning. The high-level outline is as follows:

- Create a risk management plan

- Identify the risks

- Perform qualitative risk analysis

- Perform quantitative risk analysis

- Plan risk responses

Designing a comprehensive risk management strategy can be a costly undertaking when it is done according to the *PMBOK*. Justification for doing a comprehensive risk management plan becomes clear only after you perform the quantitative risk analysis, in which hard-dollar figures are assigned to the risks. It is like the chicken and egg causality dilemma.

The traditional approach works well when planning for business risks. Business risks are external to the Agile software development world.

Agile, by virtue of its iterative nature, can be thought of as a "self-healing" environment when it comes to managing negative technical risks. Negative risks can be mitigated by addressing risky technical assumptions early in the project. This gives the team time to wrestle with the problem and experiment with various solutions. A small proof-of-concept project is a good mechanism for experimenting with risky code; the risky code can be fully developed and debugged without breaking the main line production code.

Agile, by virtue of its iterative nature, is well suited to take advantage of positive risks. A *positive risk* is one that moves you toward a desired goal or opportunity. Often, as mentioned earlier, new and better ideas pop up during development as the developers learn about the business and the business users learn about the technology. Synergy is a wonderful thing to observe and in which to participate. It is fun and invigorating. Adjusting a plan based on new and better ideas usually leads to a better product as long as the overall cost and schedule are kept within reasonable bounds.

Procurement Management: Planning

Procurement, in the software industry, involves the purchase of third-party software and hardware. Traditional project management processes handle this very well. Agile does not speak to procurement management.

Executing

The executing process group is the place where developers live. This is where they do the professional thing that they love, building high-quality valuable software. This is the process group in which the high-level project plan is diced into small iterations that are organized and run as micro-projects. Each micro-project, or iteration, itself incorporates all five process groups: initiating, planning, executing, monitoring and control, and closing. The five process groups, of course, are run in an extremely compressed fashion at this level, with very little formality.

The executing process is like stepping on the accelerator in our Formula One race car analogy. We point the car in a direction and go.

Integration Management: Executing

Traditional integration management in the executing process group encompasses a wide range of activities. The project manager handles activities that involve external teams that are not directly involved in software development. Examples are as follows:

- Managing staff

- Acquiring materials, tools, equipment, and facilities that are needed

- Managing external communication channels (status reports to management, etc.)

- Manage sellers and suppliers

The development team handles all aspects of developing code. Examples are as follows:

- Create project deliverables

- Implement the planned methods and standards

- Generate project data such as actual time to complete a task and task status

- Collect and document lessons learned

Agile's principle of "*self-organizing teams*" kicks in here.

Quality Management: Executing

Managing quality is a joy to most dedicated developers. In this context, managing quality entails building working software that is built in accordance with the team's standards that are embodied in its rules and guidelines document (see Chapter 7).

Human Resources Management: Executing

Earl Weaver, manager for baseball's Baltimore Orioles, once said, "It's easy to manage when you have good players." This is especially true in the Agile software development environment, where you have a team of skilled and highly motivated developers who actively contribute on a "*self-organized team*" that is supported by management that believes and acts on the principle that "*projects are built around motivated individuals, who should be trusted.*" In this environment, the team takes care of itself with little formal input from the project manager. The project manager is involved only when new resources need to be found and added to the team or when team members are finished and need to be moved on to other projects.

Communication Management: Executing

Communication management during the project executing process consists of, well, communicating. The project manager is responsible for keeping all of the external stakeholders informed of the project's progress. External status reports can be done on a daily, weekly, or monthly basis depending on the individual stakeholders' needs and roles.

The accuracy and reliability of the project manager's status reports depend heavily on the developers' care and attention to recording the actual time they spent on a task and the developers' honesty when reporting their progress on a task. This area of communication between the developers and the project manager is one where tension can exist. Developers can tend to procrastinate when it comes to time recording. Developers can tend to resort to green shifting when reporting their progress on a task. Green shifting refers to the human tendency of avoiding reporting bad news. In a software context, developers will often report a task as green, meaning it is on schedule, when it is, in fact, behind schedule or should be classed as yellow. The same shift is applied when a task should be classed as red, meaning that a deadline will be missed; the developer reports it as yellow, meaning it is only behind schedule. Green shifting drives project managers nuts because they end up with a lot of egg on their faces when a task that has been reported as green for two weeks suddenly turns up red on the last day of an iteration. This nasty surprise raises the blood pressure of everyone involved and erodes any sense of trust between parties involved in the project.

Agile helps guard against green shifting through the daily stand-up meeting. If a piece of working software is starting to slip, it will be noticed early in the iteration. Remedial action can then be quickly taken to get the task back on track. Agile also recommends that the team's progress be published on a public chart that is highly visible to the team. This encourages the team members to record their elapsed time and task status immediately when a task is completed.

APEX's team development module helps in this area by making it easy to enter high-level tasks in the To Do repository and easy to update the actual elapsed time and current status with just a few mouse clicks and keystrokes.

Procurement Management: Executing

Procurement management, during the executing process, consists of buying and installing third-party software and hardware. This task is outside the Agile environment.

Monitoring and Controlling

The monitoring and controlling process is concerned about where we are, how we got here, and where we go next.

The monitoring and controlling process is like steering in our Formula One race car analogy. We are constantly making adjustments to the car's direction to keep it on the road. We use the lessons learned on previous corners to help us navigate through the corners that are coming up.

Integration Management: Monitoring and Controlling

Traditional integration management in the monitoring and controlling process group is concerned with ensuring that the project conforms to the original project plan. When a project veers from the original project plan, steps are taken to record the changes via a change control process, whereby the original plan documentation is amended to reflect the changes.

One of Agile's core values is *"responding to change over following a plan."* This sounds like heresy to a traditional project manager; however, it is a reality in the software industry. An Agile project starts out knowing that it will probably not conform to the high-level plan 100% of the time and that following a plan doggedly in spite of obvious changing conditions is foolish. An analogy could be a road trip from New York to the West Coast—Seattle, for example. We start out thinking we should get to Seattle via a northern route. On the way, we hit a snowstorm and veer to the south to avoid it. In doing so, we find ourselves going through Dallas instead of Chicago, and by doing so we discover that we like warmer weather over the cold. Since we are already on a southern course, we decide to change our goal to San Francisco because it is warmer than Seattle. Going further we find our way blocked by the Rocky Mountains and decide it will take too much fuel to traverse them. Again we head south to avoid the mountains and find ourselves going through Nevada, which is not just warm, but hot. We like it and adjust our final goal from San Francisco to San Diego. In the end, we have reached the high-level goal of reaching the West Coast. In changing our plans on the fly, we have avoided a snowstorm, which would have slowed us considerably, and avoided traversing high mountains, which would have increased our fuel costs. In the end, we ended up in a lovely and warm city on the West Coast, which is a much better place for us to be (my apologies to Seattle, which is, in fact, a lovely city albeit a bit rainy in the winter).

Scope Management: Monitoring and Controlling

Scope management in the monitoring and controlling process group consists of the following:

- Verifying scope
- Controlling scope

The project customer verifies scope by accepting the software products as they are delivered.

Scope control, in an Agile context, is not too concerned when the planned features are changed or dropped or when new features are added. These changes are expected. What must be controlled, however, is the overall budget and schedule. Costs and schedule must remain close to the original, agreed-on estimates in the face of changing requirements and deliverables.

Time Management: Monitoring and Controlling

Time management, in an Agile context, is tightly related to scope management. Agile's principle of *"welcoming changing requirements, even late in development"* must be respected but respected within the scheduled amount of time. A late project is counted as a failed project.

Cost Management: Monitoring and Controlling

Cost management is done from the same perspective as time management. Changing requirements are welcomed, providing the overall cost targets are hit. An overbudget project is counted as a failed project.

Quality Management: Monitoring and Controlling

Quality management requires a great deal of interaction and communication between the development, testing, and business teams. Ideally, these three teams should be co-located so that they can take advantage of the Agile principles of "*close, daily co-operation between business people and developers*" and "*face-to-face conversation is the best form of communication.*"

The testing team is responsible for ensuring that the software works mechanically. The testing team looks for software bugs and must articulately communicate the bug details to the developers so that the bug can be reliably reproduced and fixed.

The business team is responsible for ensuring that the software fulfills the business requirements. The business team looks for flaws, omissions, and possible improvements in the requirements and design.

All three teams will find that the APEX Team Development feedback module (see Chapter 6) provides significant help with quality management by providing the teams with an efficient closed feedback loop.

Communication Management: Monitoring and Controlling

Communication management consists of reporting project performance. Upper management and external stakeholders are kept in the information loop in both the traditional and Agile worlds via status reports.

APEX's Team Development does an efficient job of producing status reports when

- The developers keep the repository up to date.

- The project manager configures Team Development effectively (see Chapter 6).

The development team uses the daily stand-up meeting to keep abreast of progress. Often, the testing and business teams are encouraged to participate in these meetings as observers. These meetings ultimately save a lot of time because the meetings can replace hundreds of e-mails over the life of a project.

Risk Management: Monitoring and Controlling

The entire project team must always be alert for the appearance of both negative and positive risks. In the traditional project management environment, risks can be overlooked and do not make themselves known until late in the project. Negative risks that surface late in a project can cause serious cost and schedule over-runs. Positive risks that surface late in a project represent lost opportunity, which can be extremely costly in a seriously competitive environment.

Agile's reliance on daily stand-up meetings mitigates the hidden risk problem. For example, the daily stand-up meeting quickly alerts the entire team to a potential risk when a developer is a day late with a task that should have taken four hours. It is hard to hide a problem in this venue. The issue is dealt with as soon as it is found, no matter if it is a developer, design, or requirements issue. The ultimate solution might not be quick if it involves a major shift in design or requirements, but at least it is out in the open, where its potential effect on cost and schedule is known.

Procurement Management: Monitoring and Controlling

Procurement management, in the monitoring and controlling process group, entails managing the procurement contracts. Did we receive the goods and services that were expected? Were the suppliers paid? These tasks are usually outside Agile's frame of reference.

Closing

The closing process group is important to the overall project as well as the individual iterations.

Integration Management: Closing

Closing a completed project is much more than just stopping work and handing the resulting product over to an operations team with a handshake. The work required is as follows:

- Transition the product to operations with appropriate training and documentation

- Obtain official and explicit acceptance from the project sponsor—this is extremely important when you expect payment for the work.

- Archive the project documentation and update the company's asset register

Closing an iteration generally involves the following:

- Review the features that were delivered

- Return undelivered features to the product backlog for future scheduling

- Conduct an iteration retrospective meeting in which team performance is evaluated and improvements are suggested

Procurement Management: Closing

All procurements must be closed at the end of a project. The company's asset register is updated, product documentation is filed properly, and suppliers are paid. This is generally handled by administrative staff and is not part of Agile software development.

Summary

This chapter's primary goal is to help developers understand where they fit in their project management environment. Their main role is to develop high-quality working software. Their secondary role, which is also important to the wider team, is to feed the project management data repository with accurate and timely data. This secondary role competes with the primary role for time; however, since the secondary role is mandatory and important, developers must take it seriously and organize their time so that the role is fulfilled quickly and accurately, so as to minimize the amount of time spent away from software development. APEX's Team Development module helps developers to fulfill their project management data entry duties quickly and accurately with a minimum of downtime.

Communicating with project managers is a fact of life. Comparing Agile to the waterfall style of project management and to the traditional view of project management gives developers the background that is required to speak in terms that resonate with a traditional project manager.

CHAPTER 6

Team Development

Team Development is a lightweight project governance tool that fits hand-in-glove with the APEX software development framework and Agile software development. Team Development is an integral part of the APEX software development framework; therefore the developers and other stakeholders do not have to spend time with inefficient context switching between APEX and an unrelated project management tool. Team Development directly complements the Agile software principles, minimizing the necessary and sometimes tedious project governance overhead.

APEX teams who take advantage of Team Development will reap the tangible rewards of increased company profitability and more personal free time—free time that can be spent on the truly important things in your life, like personal mental health, personal physical health, your family, and your social network.

Team Development consists of five modules:

- Feedback

- Features

- To Dos

- Bugs

- Milestones

Feedback is an APEX mechanism that encourages all stakeholders to collaborate with the developers in the development process. A feedback link is built into every page in an APEX application, making it quick and easy for any user to make suggestions, float ideas, and report bugs. The Feedback mechanism is built into the APEX framework; therefore it captures the user's comments plus the application's context at the time the comment is made. The latter point is invaluable to the developers. I believe that the Feedback mechanism is incredibly important because it directly supports Agile's emphasis on "customer collaboration."

Features are a list of high-level artifacts that are valuable to the project management process. The list of features tells everyone "what" is being built.

To Dos are a list of low-level tasks that assist a self-organizing team to stay organized. The team figures out what work needs to be done in order to build a feature. The work is captured in the list of to-dos; developers then check out the to-dos and work on them. The list of to-dos tells everyone "how" a feature is being built.

Bugs are kept in a list that is separate from the features and to-dos. The separation allows the bug-fixing life cycle to be handled in a versatile manner. Simple bugs are fixed quickly with no need for long-term tracking. Complex bugs may have a life cycle that spans several product releases; these might need to be tracked using a feature or a set of to-dos.

Milestones are used to coordinate the project's timeline. Features, to-dos, and bugs can all be associated with a milestone; this association is the basis for an effective report that lets everyone know what is being delivered and when it is being delivered.

Team Development was introduced to APEX in version 4. Its introduction as a marquee module is a clear sign that APEX is maturing with age. Oracle's APEX team used Team Development to manage the development of APEX version 4. Since the APEX team "ate its own dog food" by using the tool, you will find that Team Development is practical and robust.

Feedback

Team Development's Feedback module is powerful. Its power shows itself when it is used aggressively throughout a project's life cycle as a catalyst for collaboration among all of the stakeholders (see Figure 6-1). The Feedback module allows everyone who is involved with the application to quickly and easily capture an idea or flash of insight while remaining within the application's context. Remaining in the application's context allows the user to record an idea without having to navigate away from the application to go to an unrelated system. I personally have difficulty with context switching; often when I switch contexts, I lose my train of thought and the idea is lost or becomes muddled. All ideas and suggestions are recorded in the feedback repository, where everyone with the development role can review and comment on them; this is a significant benefit over having the ideas spread across several platforms. Remember, this type of close collaboration is a key cornerstone of Agile software development.

The return on investment (ROI) for Team Development's Feedback module is almost infinite. The investment time is measured in seconds or minutes, while the return time is measured in days, weeks, and potentially months. Feedback is deceptively simple, and its simplicity tends to mask its potential power.

Traditionally, many of us have viewed software feedback mechanisms as channels for reporting bugs and problems. This is a negative view that probably has its roots in our experiences with help desk ticket applications. Team Development's Feedback module is not just another help desk ticket application. It is much more. It empowers everyone who touches an application to collaborate on building better applications and better business processes. Feedback enables all of the stakeholders to share ideas from within an application, where all of the application's context is available. Feedback acts as an efficient and effective repository for the following:

- Bugs

- Problems

- Questions

- Constructive criticism

- Suggestions

- Ideas

- Insights

- Flashes of brilliance

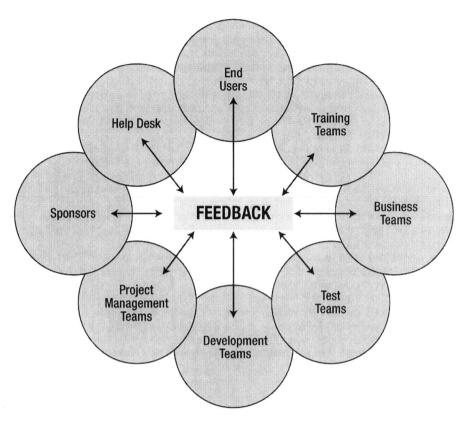

Figure 6-1. *Feedback, the collaboration hub*

The Feedback module can be used by the following:

- End users

- Help desk

- Training teams

- Sponsors

- Project manager teams

- Business teams

- Test teams

- Development teams

End users typically use an application frequently. They are the ones who are irritated by seemingly minor inefficiencies in a graphic user interface (GUI). Minor inefficiencies that add only two or three seconds to a process represent major cost savings for an organization when the two or three seconds are multiplied by several thousand users performing the process ten times a day. For example, the cost of a two-second inefficiency times two thousand users times ten inefficiencies per day times two hundred days per year times fifty dollars per user-hour times one hour per sixty seconds is over six and a half million dollars. It pays big dividends to listen to your savvy end users.

The help desk is uniquely positioned to recognize patterns in end-user behavior. Over time, the help desk can identify solutions to issues that come to them repetitively.

Training teams typically produce screenshots for their training documentation. In doing so, the training team looks at an application with fresh and critical eyes. Inconsistencies in flow and terminology, when they are found and corrected before an initial release, can reduce training time and the number of calls that are directed to the help desk.

Sponsors live in the strategic world. Project managers are concerned primarily with cost, schedule, and quality targets. Both teams will appreciate the timely and efficient reporting capabilities of the Feedback module.

The business and test teams are the first groups that get their hands on a new release of an application. They are heavy users of the Feedback module during the application construction. Both teams run the application looking for business and technical defects. When a defect is found, the Feedback module provides a fast, immediate, and accurate communication channel that enables the developers to respond quickly with a minimum number of follow-up calls and e-mails.

The business and test teams look at software products from an outside-in perspective, which is very different from a developer's inside-out perspective. The Feedback module helps to reconcile the two different perspectives through constructive collaboration.

Developers themselves are heavy users of the Feedback module. Often, a developer is working on a task and spots an issue. The Feedback module allows the developer to document the issue immediately together with all of the underlying context and session state data. The developer then continues with the task at hand with almost no interruption in the current workflow. The new issue is completely recorded in the feedback repository, where the team lead can review and classify it so that it can be addressed.

The User Perspective

From a user's perspective, the Feedback module is simple, intuitive, quick, and easy to use. A link to the Feedback page (see Figure 6-2) is automatically added to every page in an application when the Feedback module is installed and enabled.

A pop-up Feedback page (see Figure 6-3) is displayed when the user presses the feedback link. On the pop-up Feedback page, the user enters a description of the bug, problem, constructive criticism, suggestion, idea, insight, or flash of brilliance in the feedback text area. The user enters the optional data and then finishes the process by pressing the Submit Feedback button. All of the data that is visible on the page is saved to the Team Development repository together with a wealth of "under the hood" information that is invaluable to developers and impossible to capture from the users via phone or e-mail.

Figure 6-2. Feedback link on an application page

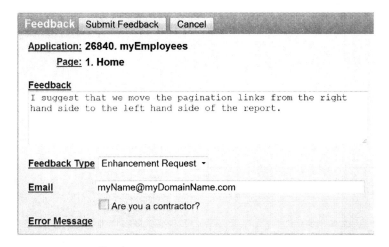

Figure 6-3. Feedback pop-up page

Feedback Flows

The previous section shows how easy it is for end users to add feedback to the Team Development repository. We will now look at the bigger picture to see how feedback and responses flow back and forth between the stakeholders.

Team Development and its Feedback module are tied to individual APEX workspaces (see Figure 6-4). Feedback data is copied from one workspace to another by the APEX import/export utility, which is used to export feedback from one workspace and import it to another. The import/export facility for feedback is identical to the familiar import/export of APEX applications (see Figures 6-5 and 6-6). The export facility creates a single file that is copied to the target environment where it is imported.

Feedback generally flows from production to test and finally to development. Responses flow in the reverse direction and can be transmitted by using the response entity that is built into the Feedback module or via e-mail to individuals or entire teams. Repetitive responses can be published on a company intranet; often the help desk is responsible for publishing repetitive responses.

Each workspace should have a feedback moderator. The moderator has a first look at all new feedback entries and is responsible for classifying individual feedback entries so they can be routed to the appropriate team.

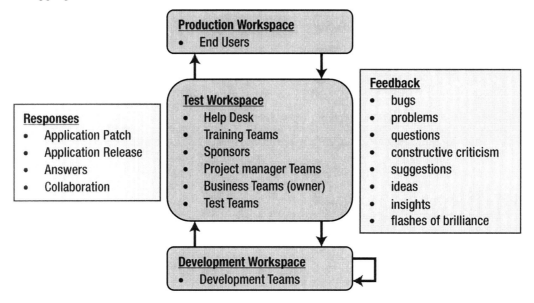

Figure 6-4. Feedback flows

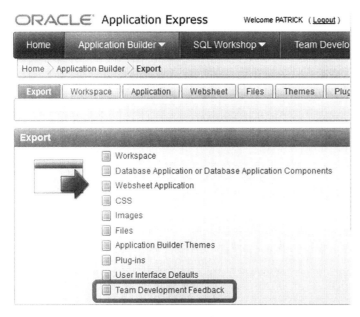

Figure 6-5. Export team development feedback

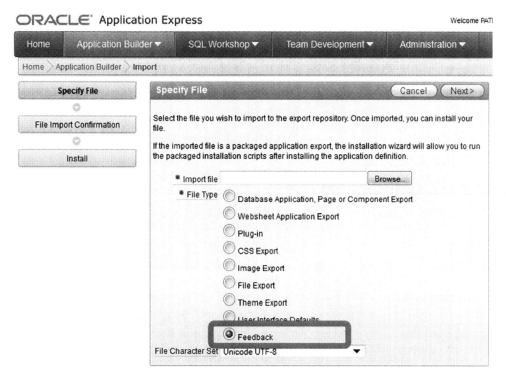

Figure 6-6. *Import team development feedback*

Feedback in the Development Workspace

Self-organizing teams can use the Feedback module to great effect during the development sprints. Individual developers are generally smart, skilled, creative, and motivated to excel. The Feedback module gives the developers a tool where a quick flash of insight can be captured and shared almost instantly with the rest of the team. Once the new insight is captured by the Feedback module, it is an item that can be put on the agenda for the next daily meeting or the next sprint kick-off meeting.

Feedback in the Test Workspace

The test workspace is home to a number of teams outside of the development sphere. I would suggest that the business team moderate this instance of the Feedback module because the business team is in the best position to classify feedback in light of the business requirements.

The test team's mandate is to run scenarios against the application to find both technical and business problems. I have had the pleasure over the years of working with a number of highly skilled and successful test teams. One thing they all had in common was a time-consuming and sometimes difficult communication process with the development team. Often, the testers captured screenshots and wrote lengthy descriptions of an issue. These communications were transmitted to the development team via an e-mail or a quality assurance application and often left out data that was critical for the development team. When critical data was left out of a communication, the issue resolution needed several back-and-forth e-mails and phone calls with a developer. In many cases, the developer could not reproduce the issue and had to leave the issue open until the issue reared its ugly head again in the future. This is never an ideal situation.

The Feedback module short-circuits the communication gap between the test and development teams. All of the APEX session state is captured in the Feedback module; therefore, laborious screenshots are not required. Feedback often gives the developer all of the data needed to re-create an issue in the development workspace.

The business team and sponsors are interested in making sure that the application fulfills all of the business requirements. Questions and observations concerning business rules, usability, and workflow are ideal inputs to the feedback repository.

Feedback in the Production Workspace

The production workspace is home to the end users. Feedback from the end users concerns itself primarily with training and business questions. The production feedback moderator could be the help desk or the business team, and, in most cases, the feedback would be answered immediately within the production context.

Occasionally, a production issue could be transported to the test workspace, where a more complex issue would be re-created and analyzed. If necessary, the issue can be passed on to the development workspace if changes to the application are required.

■ **Note** Do not move the feedback data from the production workspace to a test workspace when your production workspace contains sensitive data. Feedback records all session states; therefore, the APEX Feedback module is a major security risk if feedback is installed and enabled. If you enable feedback in a workspace containing sensitive data, your moderator must have the appropriate security clearance. Feedback data that is sent from a sensitive production workspace to a test or development workspace must be redacted or masked.

Feedback in a Project Life Cycle

Feedback usage varies significantly over a project's life cycle (see Figure 6-7).

When APEX is used as a prototyping tool, the Feedback module is used to facilitate collaboration between the development and business teams. The development team will generally cobble together a rough idea of how the application should look based on their first understanding of the business requirements document. The rough idea is often very rough and requires a lot of input from the business team. In the prototype, the overall navigation strategy is designed together with high-level process flows. As more modules are prototyped, more feedback is required. At this stage, one must remember that the Feedback module is merely a tool that supports the people. It is still important for the teams to meet face-to-face during this stage in the project life cycle. Often, feedback entries will be made at times when the developers and the business team are sitting side-by-side. These feedback entries capture design decisions and can act as concise and effective meeting minutes.

Feedback usage remains very high when the first version of the working software is delivered to the test workspace. Here, the test team joins the fray. At this point, the test team will aggressively use the Feedback module to document technical and business defects. The business team will second-guess some of the decisions that were made in the prototype; often a few areas in the prototype will be reworked after the working software shows that the original design is actually a bit awkward to use. This is a natural example of the iterative and agile nature of software development.

As development unfolds through multiple iterative sprints, feedback usage should decline. This is due to the fact that the business team progressively learns more and more about the capabilities of the development team and the development tools. It is also due to the fact the development team learns more and more about the business environment. The progressive learning on both sides makes each iterative sprint more productive because more and more software is delivered defect-free.

When the first release is delivered to production, there will be an initial flurry of feedback activity while the end users come up to speed. This activity declines rapidly and settles to a low level that comes from new end users and the occasional insightful suggestion from a savvy user for an incremental improvement.

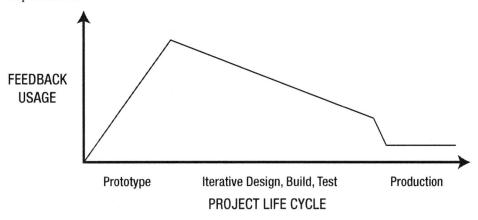

Figure 6-7. Feedback usage over a project's life cycle

Team Development Architecture

Team Development is simple, extensible, and flexible. These properties make it an ideal fit with Agile.

Simplicity, which is one of the twelve underlying principles of Agile, is illustrated in Figure 6-8. There are only six major entities: Features, Milestones, To Dos, Bugs, Feedback, and Response. Each entity has a rich set of attributes that are used to manage and track the development of a product and the progress of the related project. Simplicity makes it easy for a team to keep the Team Development repository up to date as the work on an application progresses.

Workspaces can contain one or many applications. When many applications are developed in a single workspace, Team Development's usage of interactive reports makes managing multiple applications relatively easy by allowing the users to filter the Team Development repository by application. The filtered reports can be saved; this allows users to customize their Team Development environment to suit the users' roles. For example, a developer could have two reports listing to-do items, one that lists the tasks that have been assigned to her and one that lists the tasks that have been assigned to the team. The ability to quickly customize reports to suit specific needs supports Agile's principle of self-organizing teams.

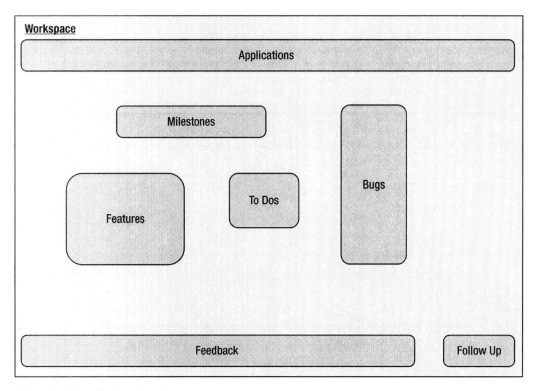

Figure 6-8. *Feedback—simple*

Features and To Dos both can have children, grandchildren, great-grandchildren, and so on (see Figure 6-9). This feature makes Team Development extensible. Features, which are used to describe the product, can be subdivided many times as a high-level design becomes more and more detailed. Eventually, a point is reached where all of the features that describe a product are clearly listed and articulated. Those of you who choose to use feature-driven development as your Agile methodology will find the Team Development's Features module to be a comfortable fit.

The extensibility of To Dos is analogous to Features. An individual task can be broken down into its sub-tasks. This allows a team lead to manage the team efficiently and effectively.

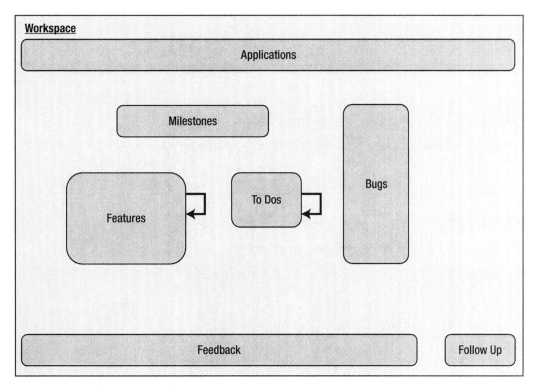

Figure 6-9. Feedback—extensible

Team Development's flexibility is illustrated in Figure 6-10. The entities can be interrelated in many ways. Teams can tailor the interrelationships to their specific needs and styles of getting the work done.

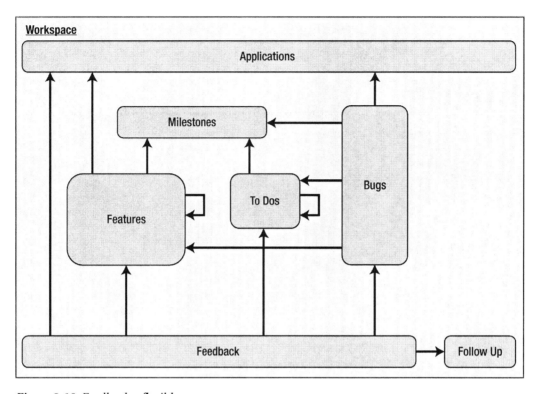

Figure 6-10. *Feedback—flexible*

You might question the need to use all of the entities and relationships in Team Development. The question is a good one because Agile values results more than process. Figure 6-11 shows an extreme programming view of Team Development. In this case, a team has taken the strategic stance of doing the simplest thing that will work. It shows that it is possible to govern a team by using only the Feedback and Feature entities. I don't recommend this as a best practice; it merely illustrates one of many strategies that teams can devise to govern their software development efforts.

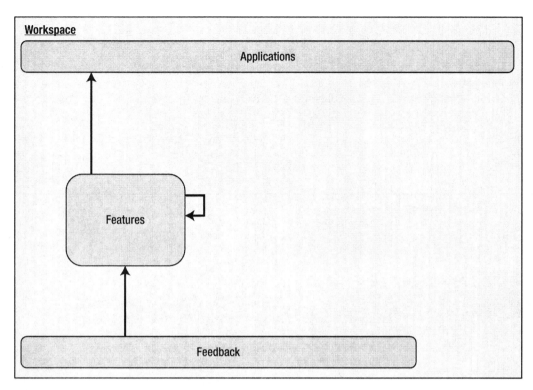

Figure 6-11. Feedback—extreme

Features

Features have two main goals. First, they are used to describe the product that is to be built. Second, they are used to track the project's progress.

Features are used at the beginning of a project to describe the high-level things that a software product must do. The initial high-level list of features is the first attempt by the development team to translate a business requirements document into web pages on top of an underlying database. The list of features is expanded to the point where budgetary estimates can be made of cost, schedule, and resource requirements. Agile values responding to change over following a plan; however, the plan has value. In fact, the initial high-level plan is mandatory for getting the money, resources, and permission to start the project. At this point, you hope that the budgetary estimates are robust enough to accommodate the inevitable plan changes that Agile predicts will happen.

Agile uses working software as the principal measure of progress. Features divide the software product into pieces that are the visible building blocks of the software product. As each feature is completed, concrete progress is reported to the sponsor and, more importantly, demonstrated to the sponsor.

Agile encourages *"sustainable development, able to maintain a constant pace."* This Agile principle guides the amount of subdivision that is applied to features. You want to be able to complete one or more features within a single two- to four-week sprint. Right-sizing the features so that they fit within the sprint time boxes enables the development team to work with a sense of steady rhythm and gives everyone a sense of progress and accomplishment. Progress and accomplishment are key motivating factors for the development team as well as the other stakeholders.

Milestones and Releases

A key Agile principle that is shared among all of the lightweight methodologies is "*working software is delivered frequently (weeks rather than months).*" Milestones and releases are ideal tools for scheduling regular delivery of working software to both the test and production environments.

Milestones can also track other events that are not directly associated with a sprint—for example, a key milestone could be the delivery of hardware that is part of a project. However, in the Agile context, a milestone's chief duty is to define a scheduled release.

Milestones and releases are closely related in Team Development. They often describe the same event. Milestones have metadata that describes the milestone event. Releases, on the other hand, are merely labels that are used to filter Team Development reports. I have found that giving a milestone and its related release the same name helps organize this area and minimizes confusion among the developers and stakeholders (see Figure 6-12). In an environment that contains many applications, it can also be helpful to add an application prefix to the milestone and release names. This strategy helps keep reports explicit and clear.

Figure 6-12. Milestone and release naming suggestion

Features, to-dos, and bugs have their due dates. Do not confuse or mix the due dates with the milestone dates. Most often, the due dates are set well in advance of the milestone's date.

To-Dos

To-dos are tasks. To-dos, like features, can be subdivided into child and grandchild to-dos. To-dos are subdivided until the lowest level where reportable control is exercised.

Two of the Agile principles are supported directly by to-dos: *"projects are built around motivated individuals, who should be trusted"* and *"self-organizing teams."* Teams have a meeting at the beginning of each sprint or iteration. During this meeting, the team decides which to-dos are to be attached to the sprint's release milestone. Once the list is finalized, it becomes the sprint backlog. Developers decide among themselves who will take on individual to-dos. The developers check out their to-dos and begin work. The daily stand-up meeting is used to constantly check progress and quickly identify any to-do that is giving someone trouble.

On average, most to-dos should require no more than a few hours to complete. Occasionally, a to-do might require several days. Team Development's to-do technology accounts for longer to-dos by tracking percentage complete and status. The overhead involved in administering the to-dos is minimal due to the fact that a link to the developer's list of to-dos is embedded in the APEX Application Builder. Check-in and check-out in this efficient environment take but a few seconds.

To-dos have a progress log that is handy for situations where more than one developer works on a to-do. The progress log acts like a diary where developers can leave notes and technical suggestions to one another. This is handy when the developers are not co-located and are in different time zones.

Bugs

Bugs are a painful fact of life. Bugs come from two main sources. The obvious source is a coding error due to a mistake or a misunderstanding of a business requirement. The other main source is an error in the business requirements document or in the underlying design.

Coding errors, when found, are generally easy to fix. In the Team Development environment, a simple bug is attached to a single to-do. The to-do is attached to a release. The to-do pops up in the release's sprint log, and a developer assigns it to himself. The fix is made and published with the next application release.

Errors in the requirements or design are potentially more problematic. Sometimes the solution requires changes to the application's entity relationship model, which, in turn, ripple through the application pages and workflow. The solution might span several sprints when the changes are large. This situation can be managed effectively by attaching the bug to a single parent to-do. The detailed work is meted out to child and grandchild to-dos that can be released over several sprints.

Developer Workflow

The Team Development repository, when it is kept up to date, is an effective and efficient source of information for all of the stakeholders. Two features of Team Development make it easy for the developers to keep Team Development up to date and make it easy for all stakeholders to extract the information that they need.

Developers are able to easily keep the Team Development repository up to date because Team Development is embedded intimately in the APEX Application Builder. Figure 6-13 illustrates the upper-right area of an APEX edit page. There are four links to the to-do, bug, feedback, and comment pages in Team Development. Clicking one of the links takes you directly to the related Team Development interactive report that is pre-filtered to the current development context (see Figure 6-14). The quick and convenient navigation between APEX's Application Builder and Team Development makes keeping the Team Development repository up to date a painless task that can easily be done in real time as part of a developer's hourly workflow.

Figure 6-13. *Team Development is intimately embedded in the APEX Application Builder.*

Figure 6-14. *To Do page pre-filtered with the context from the Edit page*

Reporting

Team Development's repository is exposed through interactive reports. This is not a trivial statement. Interactive reports allow all of the stakeholders to easily customize a set of reports that are meaningful to their work.

Developers will quickly build interactive reports that show their personal to-dos for the current sprint. A report showing the sprint backlog allows them to quickly take charge of their next to-do. Team leads or scrum masters probably will customize reports for both the sprint backlog and the product backlog.

Progress reports are of interest to the sponsor and business teams. Progress reports can be customized for both groups by using the interactive report on the Features page.

Figure 6-15 shows you the to-do report's default columns on the right-hand side of the shuttle. The left-hand side of the shuttle contains all of the other metadata that is available for inclusion in the report. All stakeholders, with a small amount of training, will quickly learn to build the reports they need for their daily, weekly, and monthly reporting and workflow control needs.

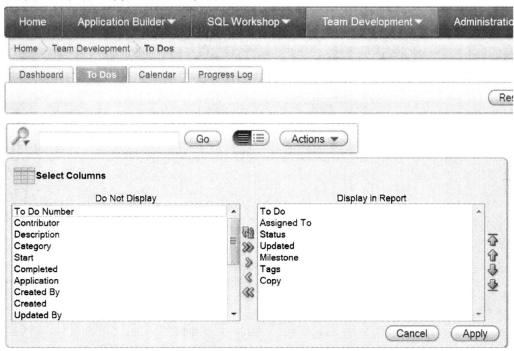

Figure 6-15. To Do interactive report, customization possibilities

Summary

Team Development is a lightweight project governance tool that is ideally suited to an Agile approach to APEX software development.

The Feedback module, when used aggressively by all stakeholders, is an ideal collaboration tool that enhances the Agile principle of *"close, daily co-operation between business people and developers."* The Feedback module can be used as a catalyst for collaboration throughout the entire software development life cycle, from proof of concept to prototype to development to testing and validation to production.

Team Development is embedded in the development fabric of APEX. This framework's convenient and efficient navigation strategy makes it extremely easy for developers to keep the Team Development repository up to date on a real-time basis. Meaningful reporting, therefore, is a snap for the entire community of stakeholders.

CHAPTER 7

Rules and Guidelines

Everyone agrees that software development standards are a good thing. Standards have tangible benefits that accrue to companies and individual developers. A standards-based company is more profitable than its disorganized competitors. Standards-based developers are more efficient; they meet their professional targets on schedule, which allows them to spend more time on the important things in life, like family, friends, and personal health.

Unfortunately, many software development shops talk about standards but never actually implement them. There are many and varied excuses as to why this is true, including these:

- Developers are not writers.

- Developers see developing standards as a huge, time-consuming project.

- Developers have higher priorities; standards development sits at priority three or four forever.

- Developers fear that standards will restrict their creativity.

- Developers fear conflict with their colleagues.

Formatting standards as terse and concise rules and guidelines is a practical way of overcoming these excuses. Developers can easily be trained to write short, active-voice sentences; this is not hard. A Rules and Guidelines document can be built in a relatively short time by adhering to Agile's core value of delivering working results on a regularly scheduled basis. A development team can make the development of rules and guidelines a realistic priority by scheduling weekly one-hour meetings that are time bound and that have an explicit agenda.

Creativity is not stifled by adhering to standards; rather, creativity is enhanced when a group of intelligent, skilled, and motivated developers brainstorm the best way to solve a problem.

Constructive conflict requires emotional maturity. Rugby and American football players start every game knowing that half the bruises they receive during the game will be inflicted by their own teammates. Software development is no different; developers will offer up solutions and ideas during a software development project and will be hurt when those ideas are rejected or altered extensively by the team. Emotional maturity allows a developer to take the hit and get on with playing the game. The bottom line is that the goal of adopting software standards is realistic and achievable.

This chapter presents a practical plan for formulating team standards by developing a Rules and Guidelines document. A cost/benefit analysis will help your team justify the effort to management. An easy-to-use format is presented as a template. Some examples are presented to help your team get its standards up and running quickly. Finally, a few words are added that discuss the tradeoff between the need for consistency and the need for change.

■ **Note** Rules and guidelines are not specific to APEX or Agile. Rules and guidelines are used in all team environments; in teams sports they are called a *play book*. This chapter uses APEX and Agile to illustrate the concept of rules and guidelines and suggests a format that is useful and practical in the APEX software development context.

Why Develop a Rules and Guidelines Document?

One of the four core values of the Agile Manifesto is to value "working software over comprehensive documentation." In all Agile areas, you must constantly remind yourself of the manifesto's caveat "while there is value in the items on the right, we value the items on the left more." Indeed, documentation has value; you need to think about why and how to develop documentation that has significant practical value in a cost-effective manner. The term *cost effective* implies that the effort expended on documentation does not impair the production of high-quality working software; rather, it enhances the production of high-quality working software so the team adheres to the Agile principle of "continuous attention to technical excellence and good design."

Benefits

Consistency is the high-level goal of using a Rules and Guidelines document. Consistency spawns many benefits that directly affect the bottom line of software development. Consistency is key to achieving the following Agile principles:

- *"Working software is delivered frequently (weeks rather than months)"*: Rules and guidelines define how a team codes an individual programming situation. In many cases, there are a number of ways to solve a particular problem; a rule or guideline cuts the number of ways down to one. This strategy stops programmers from continually reinventing wheels and dithering over the best way to do simple, low-value, repetitive tasks. The time savings are significant.

- *"Continuous attention to technical excellence and good design"*: Authoring your Rules and Guidelines document is a team sport. Chances are that, given input from multiple knowledgeable people, you will end up with some seriously practical and cost-effective rules and guidelines that result in high-quality software and practical processes that keep the team pulling together.

- *"Simplicity"*: Using one solution to a common problem instead of five solutions leads to simple, consistent code. Using one solution versus five solutions cuts the development, testing, and debugging times dramatically.

- End users love a consistent interface. It saves training time. It minimizes the amount of documentation they have to read. It makes them more productive because routine tasks like navigation become second nature—no more looking for the Cancel button that has been placed at various locations on an application's pages because each programmer has their own uncompromising idea regarding the button's correct position.

- *"Self-organizing teams"*: Authoring a Rules and Guidelines document is a positive team-building process. For new teams, authoring the Rules and Guidelines document will quickly lead them through the classic team-building steps of forming, storming, norming, and performing. Strong teams emerge from the team-building process when it is done in a spirit of cooperation, compromise, emotional maturity, and constructive conflict.

- *"Regular adaptation to changing circumstances"*: Refactoring code in response to changing requirements and technology is easier and much faster when a consistent strategy was applied to the code in the first place.

A practical and effective Rules and Guidelines document keeps your team pulling together in the same direction just as an eight-person rowing team coordinates each pull on their oars so their racing boat glides quickly and smoothly through the water toward the finish line. In an oared racing boat, team members put aside their own individual rowing style and conform to the team's rowing style. You can easily picture what happens when one oarsman rows at five strokes per minute and another rows at six strokes per minute; the result is a slapstick comedy. Team-based software development is no different. Each team member must put aside their individual style and agree to pull together using the team's style. A well-crafted Rules and Guidelines document is an ideal tool for defining a team's winning style.

Costs

A Rules and Guidelines document is not free. The main cost is developer time. In one project I was involved with, I measured the effort expended to develop the rules and guidelines. Here are the results:

- 4 developers

- 12 one-hour meetings over 3 months

- 2 hours per meeting to polish and format the Rules and Guidelines document

- 72 person-hours to develop the initial draft

During the first year, the team evolved and so did the rules and guidelines. The evolution was in line with Agile's principle of responding to change. The team held regular reflective learning meetings that were specifically dedicated to reviewing the rules and guidelines. Some items were added, some dropped, and some improved. The cost involved in maintaining the Rules and Guidelines document for one year worked out as follows:

- 4 developers

- 7 one-hour monthly meetings that were held after the first 3 months of initial development

- 2 hours per meeting to polish and format the Rules and Guidelines document

- 42 person-hours to evolve and improve the rules and guidelines

The total cost of the rules and guidelines in the first year was 114 person-hours. This cost reflects the formal time spent working on the rules and guidelines. There were, of course, hours spent on informal chats and debates over coffee and beer. The informal hours were not included because they were not captured by the time-entry system; however, informal time is an important part of collaboration and team building. A wise manager sets up the team environment to support both formal and informal time.

Return on Investment (ROI)

I calculated the amount of time saved by applying rules and guidelines during the first year of development and production usage of the same application that I mentioned in the preceding section. That application was constructed by four developers. Following is a summary of the time saved as a result of having a clear Rules and Guidelines document:

- Developer time saved:

    - 4 developers times

    - 5 minutes saved per working day times

    - 200 working days in a year equals

    - 67 developer-hours saved per year

- End user time saved:

    - 280 end users times

    - 1 minute saved per working day times

    - 200 working days in a year equals

    - 933 end user hours saved per year

Approximately 1,000 person-hours were saved in the first year by virtue of having a Rules and Guidelines document in place that produced an application that was consistent for both the developers and the end users.

The return on investment (ROI) in this example is 1,000 person-hours of benefit divided by 114 person-hours of cost. This yields an ROI of 877 percent. Even if the benefit estimate is overstated, it is clear that a Rules and Guidelines document makes an immediate positive contribution to your bottom line.

Audience

Who reads the Rules and Guidelines document? The development team is the obvious key user group. However, the rules and guidelines are of interest to a wider audience:

- Developers

- Auditors

- Business analysts

- Estimators

- End users

Developers are both the authors and the primary readers of their Rules and Guidelines document. Rules and guidelines are written directly for the developers and for no one else; however, other people in different roles will greatly appreciate that the rules and guidelines exist and are taken seriously.

Auditors are charged with making sure value is received for money. In a software development shop, this function can be difficult because of the complicated and often obscure nature the software environment. A Rules and Guidelines document shows the auditors that the development team spends much of its time on well-defined tasks that explicitly contribute to reaching well-defined goals. Well-defined tasks have well-defined time estimates associated with them; therefore, the auditors can, for the tasks governed by rules and guidelines, calculate value for money.

Business analysts find rules and guidelines handy when they are learning what the underlying technology can do for them and their end users. This saves time.

Estimators can take advantage of rules and guidelines by being able to associate a specific rule or guideline with a specific function point in an application. For example, if a proposed feature contains ten lookup tables, and a guideline standardizes the method of building the maintenance pages and related lists of values, then it is a simple matter of multiplying the guideline estimate by ten and adding the result to the overall estimate for the feature. This method is not a panacea for making good estimates; rather, it is a quick way to efficiently quantify much of the routine work associated with software development. Quickly accounting for the routine stuff frees the estimator's time so that more effort is available for the difficult areas to be estimated.

End users will probably never directly see or read the Rules and Guidelines document. However, they indirectly see and experience the benefits when they are presented with a suite of applications that has a consistent style, look and feel, and architecture. A good example is Microsoft Office: users can switch back and forth between the product's various modules and find that common elements like file management and printing are found in the same place and are named identically. Consistency like this makes the end user productive.

Structure

The following structure for a Rules and Guidelines document is simple and effective:

- Table of contents
- Environment
- Principles
- Rules
- Guidelines

Table of Contents

A table of contents is useful for any technical document. Readers can jump straight to the part that they need; this saves time. It is always surprising to me when I find in-house documentation that lacks this helpful and easy-to-create feature.

Most of us think of a table of contents in the context of a traditional document authored in a word processor. In today's world, I strongly recommend that you use an online tool to author your rules and guidelines. Websheets, a marquee feature of APEX 4.0, is an ideal tool for this purpose. The table of contents in this environment becomes a list of links on a home page.

Environment

A brief description of your overall environment helps to keep your rules and guidelines within reasonable boundaries. Your environment is the context that guides decisions of how to deliver software solutions to your customers. A typical environment might be described as follows:

- We are an oracle shop with 20 developers.

- We have 15 senior developers and 5 junior developers.

- Our main tools are Oracle Forms and Oracle Application Express (APEX).

- Over time, we will migrate Oracle Forms to either APEX or ADF, or perhaps a mixture of both.

- We have approximately 2,000 end users scattered throughout approximately 93 departments.

- We publish company information on an external web site.

- Team technical skills:

  - Oracle Forms—Expert

  - Oracle Portal—Expert

  - PL/SQL—Expert

  - SQL—Expert

  - APEX—Proficient

  - BI Publisher—Proficient

  - JavaScript—Novice

  - ADF—Novice

  - AJAX—No knowledge

  - jQuery—No knowledge

It is important to be honest in describing your environment. The environmental description will guide you as you develop your principles, rules, and guidelines. It will also guide you as you look to the longer term and will influence your future training plans and technology acquisitions.

Principles

A clear and articulate statement of your team's principles together with the reasoning behind the principles helps you to proactively manage your customers' expectations. For example, you might adapt the agile principle of simplicity and create a more specific version of that principle for your current project:

> *We will minimize the work done and the client's costs by not expending effort on code to support features that we believe the client might possibly request some day, but that are not currently in the requirements for the project.*

The goal here would be to apply the Agile principle of simplicity specifically to the issue of whether you create hooks now for nice-to-have features that might or might not be requested years down the road.

Your client's expectations are often formed by a small number of sophisticated applications that have been developed over many years at the cost of hundreds of millions of dollars. Most companies, even large ones, cannot match the software-development budgets of Oracle and Microsoft. Your statement of principles enables you to negotiate from a position of strength when clients come to you with requests and suggestions that would pull you away from your efficient and cost-effective way of developing software.

Rules

Rules are to be followed 100 percent of the time with no exceptions; therefore, the rules section of your Rules and Guidelines document should be very short. Many developers do not like to be forced into a box; however, when the reasons for the rules are clear and are clearly beneficial, most developers are happy to conform—at least, that has been my experience, with only a very few exceptions.

The specific rules that govern a team are unique to each team; much depends on the team's environment. Candidate topics for rules could be

- Naming conventions for Oracle database objects

- APEX item validations

- Error handling

- Code instrumentation

- Using APEX lists for navigation instead of APEX tabs

- Authentication

- Authorization

- Page security

Keep the long-term ROI in mind when authoring your rules. A rule must deliver high value throughout the entire software life cycle.

Guidelines

Guidelines are to be followed approximately 90 percent of the time. Most well-engineered software takes advantage of patterns, and most situations fit neatly into these patterns. Like rules, guidelines keep programmers productive and the software consistent. Most of the time, programmers will apply the guidelines to their work in exactly the same manner as the rules.

Adopting guidelines in a team environment requires compromise, which, in turn requires emotional maturity on the part of team members. Seemingly trivial group decisions can cause a great deal of potential conflict. I worked in one shop where the number of indentation spaces in code was a major bone of contention. This illustrates the fact that some developers can have very strong opinions and can be very passionate about how to do things the "right" way. A passion for excellence is a good thing, but it must be tempered by a healthy dose of pragmatism and at times, uncomfortable compromise.

Every team will come up with its own unique set of guidelines. Here are a few examples. APEX offers many choices when creating a validation on an item. A guideline could limit the number of choices when selecting a PL/SQL validation. The guideline could recommend using the "Function Returning Boolean" option and ignore other three options. A guideline could recommend using the "Reports Region 100% Width" template for all report and forms regions. A guideline could recommend horizontal list regions for tab-like navigation across the top of a set of pages replacing the need for APEX tabs. A guideline could recommend the preferred way to trap and report PL/SQL errors in an APEX PL/SQL autonomous block. The number of possible guidelines is infinite; teams must choose wisely and not micro manage trivial parts of their software development environment. Good judgement in this area is mandatory and it is always good to remember the Agile prinicple of *"simplicity"*.

░ **Note** An example of a *rule* is that you should always stop your car at a red traffic light. An example of a *guideline* is that someone walking at night should carry a flashlight and wear reflective clothing. The difference is sometimes subtle, and sometimes the distinction is the result of an arbitrary decision that you choose to make.

Exceptions always exist. They must be brought up in the team's daily meeting. The team must throw ideas around to see if the exception can be restated so it fits into the guideline framework. When the exception is accepted as a true exception, then the team brainstorms a solution. The solution is coded together with the appropriate level of comments. Commenting the exceptions is always mandatory—in other words, doing so is a rule.

Publication

I strongly recommend the following suggestions for publishing individual rules and guidelines:

- Use one page per rule or guideline.
- Use standard headings.
- Use short, terse, concise, active-voice sentences.
- Use screenshots generously.
- Use APEX's Websheet tools to author a web-based document in a Wiki format.

Having one rule or guideline per page makes the document modular. This strategy makes it relatively easy to adapt the rules and guidelines to individual projects through a mix-and-match process. Advocates of the Pragmatic Programming methodology will find this approach attractive because it allows teams to quickly pick the rules and guidelines that suit individual projects.

Standard headings provide a template. Templates speed up the writing process by providing a consistent framework and pattern.

Short, terse, concise, active-voice sentences are easy to write, easy to read, generally unambiguous, and use fewer words that their passive voice cousins.

Screenshots are valuable. They save a lot of writing and, in many cases, can completely replace writing when they are accompanied by terse annotations.

Publishing rules and guidelines in an APEX Websheet makes a great deal of sense when the team works almost exclusively in an APEX environment. The benefits of using a websheet are as follows:

- There is one master copy. Old, out-of-date copies do not exist.

- Websheets can be maintained by multiple authors. This is attractive in an APEX environment where multiple diverse technologies are used simultaneously. The team's technology experts can take charge of their area of expertise. The team should appoint a moderator to oversee the websheet so that consistency and clarity is maintained over the entire Rules and Guidelines document.

- Websheets are APEX centric. Therefore, the environment is already familiar to the team. The learning curve for websheets is very shallow.

- All developers can quickly and easily access the rules and guidelines websheet from within their APEX development environment by using the Links region on the Team Development home page (see Figure 7-1).

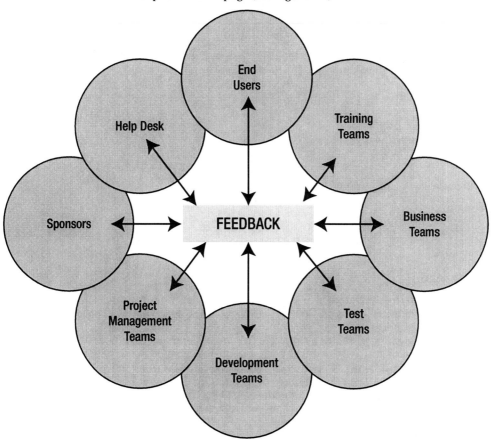

Figure 7-1. Team Development link to the Rules and Guidelines websheet

---

⬛ **Note** I was surprised at the Oracle Developer Tools User Group (ODTUG) conference, Kscope11, when nobody raised their hand when a large group of APEX developers was asked, "Who is using websheets?" I sincerely believe that when an APEX development shop takes a bit of time to develop their own websheet, they will quickly see the tremendous potential for this simple and easy-to-use tool. Publishing your Kscope11 trip reports is an extremely practical use for a websheet application. The book *Beginning Oracle Application Express 4* (Apress, 2011) contains two chapters on websheets plus a working websheet download.

Format of Individual Rules and Guidelines

Headings for individual rules and guidelines are divided into mandatory and optional sections. At least one of the optional headings is always present. The headings are as follows:

- Mandatory section
  - Title
  - Rule or guideline
  - Why
- Optional section (one optional heading is usually present)
  - Result
  - How
  - Notes
  - See Also

The Title heading contains a single word or simple phrase that describes the rule or guideline. Use this as the navigation link to the rule or guideline in a websheet. Use it as a table-of-contents entry in a conventional word-processor document.

The Rule or Guideline heading contains a simple, active-voice statement that describes the main purpose of the rule or guideline.

The Why heading can be one word: "Consistency," for example. Some rules and guidelines will, of course, require more justification. The Why heading is important for developer buy-in. It's also an important negotiating tool used when other stakeholders challenge the team's strategies. Most of your stakeholders are reasonable. You can win them over to your vision by presenting them with logical reasoning that has validity in the short and long terms.

The Result heading often contains nothing but a screenshot of the desired result. This is frequently all a developer needs. For example, experienced APEX developers know exactly how to build a horizontal navigation list that is based on images. The guideline does not need to tell them how.

The How heading is used where you need to document the details of how a result is to be achieved. You do this when

- There are multiple ways of getting to the result.

- Multiple steps are required.

- You have programmers who are not yet proficient using APEX.

- You need succession planning for periods of high programmer turn over.

- You share resources with other teams, and programmers are assigned to you for short periods of time.

The How heading is the logical place to publish code snippets that can easily be copied to the working code. This is a great time saver.

The Notes heading is used to document aspects of the rule or guideline that are not obvious. Some guidelines may have side effects. Perhaps a guideline is an imperfect solution based on a technical compromise. This heading saves time by alerting programmers to the circumstance before they waste effort solving a tricky problem that has already been explored and dealt with.

The See Also heading points developers to related rules and guidelines.

Figures 7-2, 7-3, and 7-4 illustrate how a Rules and Guidelines document looks when it has been published using APEX's Websheet tool.

Figure 7-2. Rules and Guidelines websheet with a table of contents on the home page

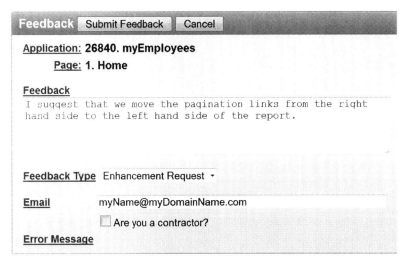

Figure 7-3. Rules and Guidelines websheet drilling down into rules

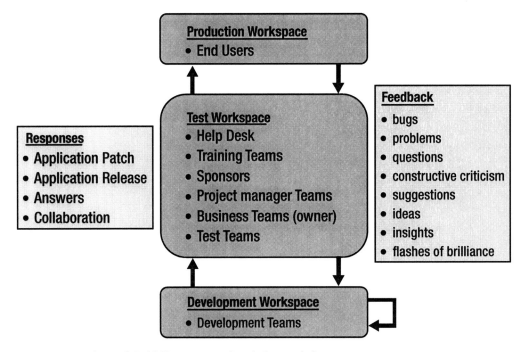

Figure 7-4. Rules and Guidelines: a sample rule in a websheet

Consistency vs. Change: Refactoring

Consistency conflicts with change. Rules and guidelines tend to favor consistency during development. Yet Agile calls for being receptive to change. How do you resolve that apparent conflict in an Agile context? The key is timing.

Consistency

Consistency provides significant value within a project. Consistency is a major factor in your ability to deliver a quality software product on time and within budget. In this context, consistency directly supports the Agile principle "Working software is delivered frequently (weeks rather than months)."

Staying with a devil you know is generally a low-risk option when you are under the gun to hit hard deadline and budget targets. Change, in this context, can be extremely risky.

Change

Change provides significant value when it improves quality, shortens delivery times, and lowers cost. Change directly supports the Agile principle "Regular adaptation to changing circumstances."

Change is risky. Change pulls your team out of its comfort zone. However, adopting change is the only way to improve. It is the only way to avoid repeating mistakes over and over again.

How does a team embrace change? Here are a few suggestions:

- Hold end-of-project reflective learning meetings. This is a core feature of the SCRUM Agile methodology.

- Budget time for research. Give programmers explicit time blocks where they concentrate on pure research for the team. Do not mix research and production time; doing so will harm both efforts.

- Research tasks must produce a tangible result. This is usually a bit of working software that demonstrates why and how a new idea can be adopted. Rejecting an idea is also a valid outcome of research.

- Start using your new tool or process at the beginning of a new project. This gives the team time to get comfortable with the change before the end-of-project crunch time adds pressure.

Refactoring

Refactoring existing code directly supports the Agile principle "Continuous attention to technical excellence and good design."

Refactoring is done only when the benefits far outweigh the costs and risk. A sub-optimal rule or guideline is acceptable when the value of consistency trumps an optimal solution whose benefit is marginal.

Refactor your existing code aggressively. Anything less will leave you with a mix of old and new ways of doing things, which defeats the pursuit of consistency. Aggressive refactoring is done by treating the refactoring task seriously and attacking it as an all-or-nothing project. Partial refactoring leads to an inconsistent environment that increases your costs and causes your users to be frustrated and to lose confidence in your ability to produce reliable and easy-to-use software.

Summary

Standards are a good thing. Think about this the next time you plug in your laptop. The power cord and the plug in the wall are beautiful examples of standards in action.

A Rules and Guidelines document is a cost-effective and efficient template that helps a software development shop to implement standards-based software development practices. Standards-based software development produces consistent software products that make developers, testers, business analysts, and end users more efficient.

Standards-based software development directly supports the goals of the Agile Manifesto and its Twelve Principles. Standards enable teams to produce high-quality working software within short scheduled time frames. Standards-based software is easier to refactor when the time comes to adopt the inevitable changes associated the rapid pace of software evolution.

I hope that you use this chapter to get started down your team's unique road to standards-based software development within an APEX and Agile framework.

CHAPTER 8

Documentation

Documentation has a bad reputation among software developers. Just mention "documentation," and those of us who were raised on traditional waterfall software project methods remember weighty requirements documents, followed by detailed design documents, followed by lengthy reviews and signoff documents, all before a line of code was written. We recall long meetings, flipping through reams of paper (the poor trees!), and the inevitable loss of enthusiasm for the project before coding even began. If we were lucky, funding (or interest) ran out before we were required to produce technical manuals, end-user manuals, operational manuals, administration manuals, and more at the completion of the coding cycle. No wonder documentation has a bad reputation for many of us aging developers—we wrote more documentation than code. Thank goodness the Agile world has left that voluminous mode of communication behind in favor of *Agile documentation*.

Agile documentation is nothing more or less than the application of Agile principles to document aspects of your software project, when and only when it is essential to do so. Agile documentation is clear, succinct, efficient, and just enough. Agile documentation can take many forms, the key factors being that it must add value and it must not cost more to produce than that value. The purpose of this chapter is to describe the principles of Agile documentation and suggest how to apply those principles to your APEX projects.

This chapter opens with an overview of the principles of Agile documentation and discusses when, how, and in what form to produce valuable artifacts that support your working software. The second part of the chapter recommends standards and habits to develop for producing Agile documentation specific to your APEX projects.

Agile Documentation

One of the core values of the Agile Manifesto is "*working software over comprehensive documentation.*" So, you say, why a whole chapter on documentation? Haven't we left that behind? While yes, the main goal *is* to produce working software. Depending on your project, it is likely that documentation in some form will be required. The difference is, in Agile software development, documentation is an essential supplement, not the driving force or the proof of completion of your project.

There is wealth of material on the topic of Agile documentation, readily available through the Agile Alliance or a simple web search, or through the reference section for this chapter. It is beyond the scope of this text to repeat that information here. It is recommended that the reader consult the chapter references for more in-depth Agile documentation material. For the scope of Agile and APEX development, the subject can be summarized in this simple statement:

Do as little as possible, as efficiently as possible, as late as possible.

To be even more succinct, the whole gist of Agile documentation can be condensed to these two words: just enough. Write just enough, and no more. Period.

Characteristics of Agile Documentation

Documentation is communication. Communication may take many forms. With today's technology, communication is more often by electronic means such as e-mail, text messaging, images, charts, and documents than by the traditional Word documents or snail mail of a decade ago.

We have instant messaging, web cams, video conferencing, Net Meeting, and Web-Ex as common meeting mediums. Preserve those communications, and we have documentation of our meetings and the information exchanged, perhaps including decisions made. We also have prepared videos, podcasts, hand-drawn diagrams, screenshots, all online instead of printed, and of course the more traditional spreadsheets, tables, and text-on-page documents. Whiteboard contents, sticky notes, a photograph of those sticky notes on a wall—all of these are valid forms of communication that may in fact document some facet of your software project. The information exchanged, how it is communicated, whether it needs to be preserved, and, if so, in what format are unique to each project. I personally consider comments in code, including APEX developer comments (the text that you should be entering in the Comments attribute of your page and region objects), as valid forms of documentation. Code and developer comments are communication of how your code (or your APEX module) works. What better place to communicate what your code is doing than in your code, where the next developer, or yourself, will see it and learn (presuming they read it!).

Before planning or producing documentation for your project, consider these factors:

- What is the least amount of information that needs to be communicated?

- What is the optimal format for that communication?

- What is the cost to produce and maintain that communication?

As Little As Possible

In Agile software methods, it is not necessary to record and preserve every fact about a software development project. It is essential to record information that is not otherwise known that is critical to the end goal of working software. If how to use a particular page of your APEX application is not intuitively obvious, communication of how to use that interface must be provided. This communication may be made in one or more of several forms: as an online help page, online tooltips on page items, an online how-to video, an online step-by-step how-to document, or an annotated user manual. Exactly what needs to be documented, and in which form of communication to provide it are decisions best made by the Agile team during the development process, following the rules and guidelines of the project and the parameters defined by the project manager.

Valid reasons to document generally fall into these categories:

- To communicate with an external group

- It is required by your stakeholders or regulatory agency.

- To define an interface with another system

- To validate a theory or thought process

- To remember

Documentation may be required to communicate during development, particularly if your team is not located together. In this case more than any other, the printed page is most costly, due to changing and evolving needs, and is the least effective. How long does it take to produce the documentation, vs. how many developers stop to read it? Consider more effective, less costly forms of communication, including screenshots, diagrams, charts, whiteboards, NetMeeting or WebEx sessions (recorded or not), or the plain old phone call—all viable means of communication when it is not possible to walk down the hall and talk face-to-face. Document only what is essential to communicate the point, in the least costly way possible.

It may be essential to produce documentation that is mandated by your organization, or by regulatory agencies in your industry. There may be an enterprise-wide requirement to produce a formal document using a corporate template, and to have all wording approved by a central communications board. In these cases, ensure the document is indeed required—that it conveys essential, valuable information about your project—and plan to deliver only and exactly what is required. You may have to produce a document, but does it have to be 12 pages, or 2? If a particular document does not add value to your project, then whenever possible get permission to not produce that document, and get that permission in writing. Be prepared to justify your request by providing the hours (and cost) to produce the documentation vs. the value added to your project (none, if you are requesting to not produce it!). In many cases, the cost vs. value added argument suffices to get a requirement waived. When you are required to complete documentation templates, the recommendation is to complete only those sections of the template that apply to your project. Again be prepared to cite the cost vs. value added evidence for sections that you are omitting, and get permission to do so in writing.

When your software is part of a contract between one system and another, documentation of the interface between the two is required. For example, if your work product is part of an API or a web service, it is necessary to document the parameters of your software in sufficient detail for others to use it. If you are consuming a web service, or accepting input data, you will need to document the expected format of the web service request or your input data format.

Sometimes you just need to put it in writing, to clarify an idea or confirm that all avenues of thought are covered. Sometimes an idea that seems clear in your mind is not so simple when drawn out on paper. Sometimes different team members envision the same idea differently, and drawing, diagraming, or otherwise documenting the concepts allows the team to work toward consensus.

Sometimes documentation is simply necessary to account for infallible memory. Do you remember details of code you wrote last year? I don't, unless I have notes to jog my memory. Through the years, I have developed a system of coding standards, comments, and notes that when combined serve to remind me of unique aspects or unusual features of a project months and even years later. This documentation, shared with others, means the why and how of my code are not lost, and it is maintainable.

If any of the foregoing reasons apply, documentation in some form will be required. Having established that documentation is communication, and there are many avenues for it, what is the best way to deliver documentation in an Agile APEX project?

As Efficiently As Possible

Once you have discerned exactly what to document, the guiding question is, what is the optimal form to most effectively communicate that information, at the least cost to the project? Figure 8-1 compares the effectiveness of various modes of communication vs. richness of content.

■ **Note** The original diagram on which Figure 8-1 is based is from Alistair Cockburn, one of the original 17 at Snowbird who pioneered the Agile movement, and a recognized expert on Agile projects and object-oriented software development. Cockburn's image was reproduced by Scott Ambler in *Agile Modeling: Effective Practices for eXtreme Programming and the Unified Process* (John Wiley & Sons, 2002). The image in Figure 8-1 is my version of the same point: modes of communication that involve face-to-face human interaction are in general more efficient than paper and non-interactive modes of communication. I took the liberty of adding text messages and web cams, two increasingly popular modes of communicating given the boom of phone technology.

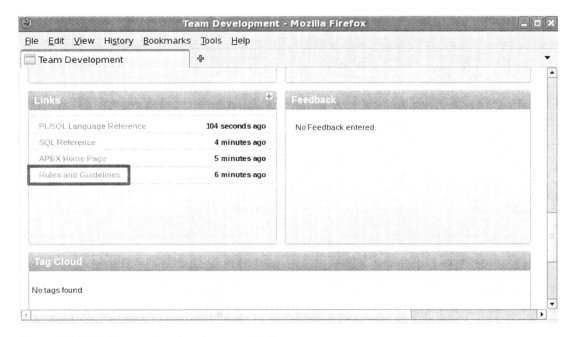

Figure 8-1. Effectiveness of modes of communication

Figure 8-1 clearly illustrates that face-to-face communication in front of a whiteboard (or similar medium) is the most effective mode of communication, while paper documentation is the least effective. Documentation options in all forms are lower on the scale than all of the modeling, less concrete options. A page of text, printed or online, is still our least effective form of communication. We should use it sparingly. We should produce text-on-page documentation only when we have to—when other forms of communication do not suffice for the particular communication need.

Notice that text messaging is missing from the chart. I suspect it will be added in future releases. My personal feeling is that text messaging, while instantaneous, falls on the low end of this scale because it lacks the verbal and visual clues that make face-to-face communication so effective. I find it interesting, and sad, that text messages and instant messages are replacing e-mails, which have replaced phone calls. Yes, text messages and e-mails document an issue, but they have no richness of content, and are therefore, in my opinion, less desirable forms of communication, even when laced with emoticons. ☹

As Late As Possible

All documents have a cost incurred to produce and maintain them. That cost to produce and maintain must be less than the value added. Documenting as late in the development cycle as possible means that fewer changes are required to keep the material up to date.

Models, diagrams, charts, drawings, and text that are part of the design evolution are best formalized only when they are stable. Stable does not necessary mean finalized, but it does mean stable. On a recent Agile project, three persons in a room drew, discussed, redrew, scribbled on, and, when satisfied they were "done," made a Visio diagram of their model to present to management. Scribbled-on drawings were fine for the development team, but not for the management meeting, where they were seeking approval to move forward. Several weeks later, the team hit a new requirement that did not fit their original model. They regrouped around the Visio model, talked out the options, and made new scribbles on the documented model until they were satisfied their revised model was correct. Then they prototyped to confirm their corrections worked, and only then adjusted their Visio model to present the updated case to management. Freehand drawings and scribbles were faster for the team during the process. Visio quickly documented the results in a format acceptable to management once the model was stable. The team formalized only at stable points in the process. The use of Visio told the story in a single picture that took one person only a half-hour to create. A Word document to formally describe the model would have taken much longer to write, much longer to present, and much longer for management to read (if they did), all incurring greater cost for the project.

As late as possible *may* mean never. In the foregoing example, if there was no need to present to management, the freehand drawings, with scribbles, would have sufficed as documentation of the model, and in that case, no Visio. If a feature is eliminated as your project evolves, the need to document goes away as well. A recent project involved a simple file upload. The uploaded file had to be in a specific format. The upload process entailed a series of validations on the uploaded records. A brief online document was planned to document the process for future users. The document was required prior to the move to production. In QA testing, the upload proved too slow. Eventually the upload was replaced by a database link—no user interaction at all, no need for the upload interface, and no documentation required. Had the development team built that documentation page in time for QA, it too would have been obsolete.

As late as possible does not always mean never. Do not mistake "as late as possible" to mean "If I procrastinate long enough I won't have to do it at all." That might happen, but the more likely reality is that the more you procrastinate, the less you are likely to have to do, which incurs less cost for your project.

Just Enough

Agile documents are clear and concise, and include just enough information, but no more. How much is "just enough"? It depends on your audience, on your stakeholders, on your contract, on your subject matter, and on your particular situation. "Just enough" for the purpose of specifying parameters for a module that controls O-ring manufacturing for the space shuttle is going to include more details than "just enough" for how to use your company's online trip report approval software. Use common sense to gauge how much is just enough in your situation. Know your subject matter, know your stakeholders, and know your industry and contractual requirements. Communicate only the essential information in the clearest, most concise format possible.

Remember that producing documentation takes developers away from producing working code—the main goal of the Agile project. Producing any more than needed, because it's nice to have, because it looks good, or for any other reason, keeps them away from coding longer. It's not worth it!

Rules for Writing

Regardless of the type of documentation—APEX help page, developer comment, item help, spreadsheet, diagram, or formal text document—I strongly recommend the following guidelines. On purpose, these are the same suggestions for publishing individual rules and guidelines in Chapter 7. Consistency across all areas of a project is nice—it promotes predictability and comfortability and can actually be habit-forming.

- Use short and concise active voice sentences.

- Write in full sentences: capitalize the first word, and place a period at the end of each sentence.

- Use clear, meaningful, full-word names for all objects.

- Use screenshots and diagrams generously.

- Consider using APEX's websheet tools to author a web-based document.

- Ensure accuracy. Few things will discourage developers from taking advantage of good documentation so much as simple lack of accuracy.

The following sections cover each of these guidelines in more detail. Follow them, and your writing will be clear and concise, and above all useful.

Active Voice and Complete Sentences

Short, concise, active sentences are easy to read, easy to understand, and easy to write. Yes, even developers can learn to write short, clear, direct, complete sentences to communicate. Pseudo-code is for code; complete sentences are for documentation. Keep the purpose and the audience of the document in mind, and provide no more and no less information than necessary. In writing documentation, you are not creating a novel; you are communicating facts about your software. Write just enough, and then stop.

Clear and Full-Word Names

The use of clear, full-word, meaningful names for all objects promotes self-documenting code at all levels, for all stakeholders. Using EMPLOYEE versus EMP removes any ambiguity (did he mean EMPty or Elector Magnetic Particle?). Meaningful names make it easier to find things when debugging. Less technical documentation is required because the code itself is clear.

ABBREVIATIONS

Short abbreviations in software have a history in the memory restrictions in the old days. Old versions of DOS, prior to Windows 95 and NT 3.51, used an 8.3 file name convention: 8 characters optionally followed by a single dot and an up-to-three-character file extension. Earlier versions of FORTRAN had a limit of 8-character variable names; FORTRAN 90 raised that limit to 31. Before that, when memory was even more expensive, programmers used single-character variable and parameter names, painfully going to two characters in very large programs because every character cost more to compile and process. I recall learning a program on my first co-op job in the early eighties, where all the variable names were A, B, C, D followed by A1, A2, A3, B1, B2, B3. I needed a cheat sheet to translate variable names into their meanings in order to begin deciphering the code. Of course the cheat sheet was not kept up to date; the veteran developers saw no need to do so, and it took actually *talking to the developers* to learn the code. Imagine that! Today, we have relatively few restrictions—Oracle's 32-character entity name limit is still with us. I consider 32 characters a gift compared to 2 or 8.3. So why do developers still abbreviate? There are several reasons:

- That's the way they've always done it.

- They want to keep their code a mystery.

- It's faster.

The first two of those excuses are plain bogus in the context of Agile development, where communication and collaboration are central. There is simply no room for "I'll do it my way" or for keeping "my way" to oneself. That selfish behavior costs the entire project.

The "it's faster" argument is also not valid. The fact that many programmers cannot touch-type is a sin. Hunt-and-peck typing short variable names is not faster if one then needs to hunt-and-peck type a full Word document to explain the code. My hope is that the next generation, weaned on video games and cell phone keyboards, will at least know how to touch-type (albeit in text message format ☺).

Images and Diagrams

A picture conveys a thousand words, and a screenshot saves typing even more. A video does even better, if you have video capture programs available. Screenshots easily convey exactly what a page in your application looks like. There is no need to describe every item on every page, or form layout or report features, if it can all be conveyed in a single screenshot. Most computers have some sort of image capture utility. When you have it, use it. Then supplement the screenshots with just enough text, using full words, to communicate the essential information.

APEX Websheets

When a team is building an APEX project, the use of APEX websheets makes sense for a number of reasons, outlined in Chapter 7. Using the Links region of the Team Development home page as a central location for all project documents, including the Rules and Guidelines document, is a wise idea. If your team is not APEX-centric, a link to an APEX websheet can be included anywhere a link is valid. At a minimum, consider adopting some form of online, central document management system, to minimize communication time, maximize communication efficiency, and maximize the return on investment of your documentation.

⬛ **Tip** Hard, offline documents, such as a Word document or spreadsheet maintained by a single user, incur a higher maintenance burden because the changes need to be communicated first, and executed, and then the updated version needs to be communicated back. All of this communicating takes time away from producing working software: it costs. Using an online document format such as APEX websheets means that all team members can have access to the documentation to perform updates and view the latest information. The online document's universal availability saves several communication steps, reducing the cost to produce and maintain the document, and increasing its return on investment.

By now you may be back to thinking about documentation as text on a page, printed or online. Let me stress again that the point of documentation is communication, and that communication can take many forms. Charts, diagrams, sketches, tooltips, online tutorials, comments in code, and videos are all forms of communication that may be acceptable for a given purpose. Traditional textbooks and hard-copy user manuals are now replaced by context-sensitive tooltips, help pages, and tutorials. Step-by-step tutorials—how-to documents—are now being replaced by YouTube videos. Take advantage of all forms of communication when choosing the most effective one for your task. Remember that not all forms of documentation are required for your project. Create only what is necessary, in the most efficient mode possible.

Be sure to match the document form with the audience. A freehand sketch of the program's workflow may be sufficient for the development team, but it is not sufficient for display to end users or management. Turn that freehand drawing into a Visio diagram and include it as an image on a help page, and you now have a non-text, effective document for your audience, at less cost than the equivalent text to describe the process in words. Use the least costly, most effective mode of communication possible to convey your information, and then stop. Just enough is enough.

Accuracy

For documentation to be of value—worth the resources you invested in its development—it needs to be clear, concise, just enough, and accurate. Inaccurate documentation in any form is worse than useless, because of the lost hours incurred in figuring out it is wrong, then in figuring out just how wrong. Besides losing resources, you lose credibility, which is much harder to reclaim. When considering the cost of documentation, include the cost of maintaining it.

Documentation Within APEX

APEX affords many avenues for incorporating documentation into your application as it is developed. The Team Development tool, when enabled for your project, tracks features, milestones, to-dos, and progress. The Application Builder contains attributes for help text and developer comments on most elements. The Application Builder Utilities offer numerous reports of your application development progress, automatically. This is a lot of information about the development activities in your application, all at no cost to your project.

If you develop wisely, use Team Development, and avail yourself of the wealth of information in the Application Builder Utilities reports, the need for additional documentation will be minimal. That certainly fits our Agile documentation criteria of doing as little as possible, as efficiently as possible. As late as possible doesn't really apply for these built-in utilities, as the reason to build documentation late is to minimize cost. As there is no cost to build or maintain the APEX tools and utilities, the only investment is in using them to discern which reports provide the most useful metrics for your particular project.

APEX Utilities

While not documentation in the traditional sense, the APEX Utilities are a valuable set of reports that document various aspects of the development of your applications. Figure 8-2 shows the APEX application Utilities home page. The help region says it all: these utilities summarize information across the application and provide access to useful tools.

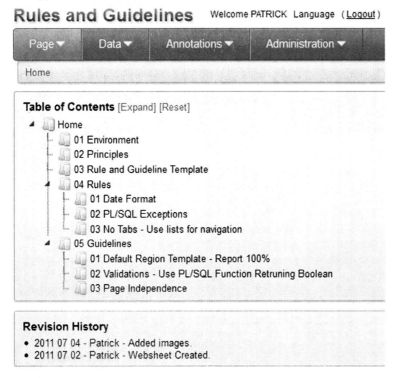

Figure 8-2. APEX Application Utilities

The data contained in the Utilities reports are all automatically collected by APEX. There is no hiding from the APEX engine—if, as a developer, you spend all day updating a page in your pet project when you were supposed to be working in another application, the APEX Utilities will rat you out, in the Change History and Recently Updated Pages reports. Curious as to the latest changes in app 107, which worked fine last week, until Teddy the Temp made a fix? Check out the Recently Updated Pages report. Need an overall health check of your application? Check out the suggestions in the Advisor. It is not within the scope of this text to describe each of these utilities, but I do recommend that all team members get familiar with them as a mode of mining information about your project, all for no added cost. That definitely fits our criteria of "as little as possible."

Team Development

The APEX Team Development tool, when used, is one way to document features, milestones, releases, to-dos, bugs, feedback, follow-up actions, and developer progress. See Chapter 7 for more complete information on Team Development features, practical use, and how it supports the core Agile values and principles.

Team Development is an ideal way to document the process and progress of an Agile development project, because it is so well integrated with the APEX application development process. The Team Development repository is exposed to APEX users as interactive reports. Developers, team leaders, and other stakeholders can customize reports to meet their needs. Developers can track their sprint backlog, or check the to-dos on the current sprint. Team leaders can monitor the sprint backlog, or prepare progress reports for business teams or other stakeholders. This simple, customizable documentation of your team development process is available with relatively little investment.

The customizable Team Development report certainly meets the criteria for Agile documentation—the report can be customized to show just enough information for the intended audience. The cost to produce the report is minimal—only the investment of entries in the Team Development interface. The only maintenance is to continue with normal entries into the milestones, releases, to-dos, and bugs interfaces. These entries would need to be recorded somewhere else, if not in Team Development, to track project progress. The wealth of valuable information output relative to the data input investment makes this lightweight form of project management a very valuable, flexible Agile documentation tool.

Standards

Standards for building an application should include standards for naming objects, standards for writing help text (which could start as database comments), developer comments, and code comments, and standards for building navigational elements. I believe that all of these are documentation—communication of some important fact about your application—even when that fact is consistency.

Here are some standards to consider that assist in documenting your application in the most agile, efficient way possible:

- Define a naming convention for pages, page items, and regions.

- Define naming and numbering conventions for pages and page groups.

- Define a naming convention for database tables and columns.

- Define naming and numbering conventions for Team Development entries.

- Define a strategy for entering feedback, developer and end-user. Developer feedback can be useful in tracking thought processes that need collaboration. Add additional feedback categories as needed.

- Define a strategy for application navigation that includes when and where to use (or not use) list menus, tabs, breadcrumbs, and navigation bar entries. Use a common convention across all of your applications.

- Mandate use of User Interface Defaults and the Attribute Dictionary to define defaults, including item help, for columns and field items.

- Define a strategy for item help that includes when and where to use tooltips, labels with help, and/or help pages.

- Define a strategy for using dynamic actions.

- Define a policy for using plug-ins.

- When additional documents are essential, define a template that includes a look-and-feel that is common to your application.

- Define a central location for all additional documents (in any form), such as the Links page in Team Development (for internal use) or links off of a help page (in your application).

The list could go on, but this is a good start. Your standards will of course vary to suit your organizational and application requirements.

Creating and applying standards for naming conventions and the use of help and comments mean that a good portion of your application is documented as it is developed. How many of us incorporate help text in every item on every form? If not, why not? For the investment of the seconds it takes to type (or cut/paste) text into a field, your end user has help for that field—as opposed to some developer (and it should be you) going back to do it later, or, worse, creating a separate document for the help. It is simply more efficient to enter the help text along the way, if it is not picked up from the Attribute Dictionary.

Creating and applying standards for look-and-feel, help format, and navigational elements mean that end users are more comfortable with your application because it is familiar—"Oh, yes, it works just like that other application that I already know how to use." Remember how you felt when Microsoft came out with the ribbon for its Office products? Now imagine if MS Word had a ribbon, and MS Excel had a detachable toolbar, and MS PowerPoint had a series of list menus, and MS Access used context-sensitive pop-up menus. There would have been a revolt! Standards for look-and-feel aspects promote consistency. Consistency promotes end-user comfortability and confidence. And that means you have less to document, because there is less new material to communicate to your users.

Standards in your APEX application should include defining User Interface Defaults and populating the Attribute Dictionary for all tables, including help text for page items. User Interface Defaults define default attributes for columns in a table that, if present, are used by the Application Builder Create Form and Report wizards. The benefit of employing User Interface Defaults is twofold: consistency (again) and saved development time. The cost incurred is the time to complete the User Interface Defaults for a table in the first place. The cost saved is the time *not* spent in manually setting attributes for each item in your form or report on subsequent create form or report actions. The invested cost is more than regained the second time you create a form or report on that table. Many developers skip defining User Interface Defaults because of the setup time. I guarantee that most of those developers are mumbling under their breath the second or third time they manually enter attribute settings for the same table—they should have used the User Interface Defaults.

Standards should also be specified for Team Development entries: naming and entering milestones, releases, features, and bugs. Milestones and releases need defined naming or numbering schemes. Features and bugs need standards for priority assignment, weight assessment, and scheduling. Naming, numbering, and priority schemes are useful only if everyone on the team uses the same conventions.

Standards for feedback—when to add it and in what category to record it in—should be included to ensure the correct feedback information is captured and forwarded to the appropriate persons.

Standards for the use of dynamic actions promote consistent page behavior and development practices. Standards for the use of plug-ins promote reuse of common features and minimize repetition of code.

Standards are essential for the development team, the stakeholders, and those who maintain the application to understand what is there, why, and how long it took to produce. Standards are also important because they promote consistency, which is in itself a form of self-documentation that aids team leaders, developers, stakeholders, and end users. There is value added in not having to go back and add information—or worse, create separate documentation. As Agile developers, we are always looking for ways to do as little documentation as possible. The use of standards helps us toward that end.

Habits

A habit is a recurrent, often unconscious pattern of behavior that is acquired through frequent repetition. My recommendation is to apply standards religiously, until they become habits.

Some habits to develop in your APEX development that promote the concepts of Agile documentation include the following:

- Use User interface Defaults.

- Use the Attribute Dictionary (import table column defaults for reuse on similar column names).

- Write developer comments consistently, using a consistent format per your organization's standards.

- Include item help as you build items, using a consistent format per your organization's standards.

- Include page help as you complete each page, using a consistent format per your organization's standards.

- Use Team Development, if enabled for your project.

- Use feedback where enabled for your project.

Note that most of these habits are in the list of standards that I recommend in the foregoing section. When standards become habits, they happen as a natural part of development and generally incur less effort. Less effort means less cost. That's what we want.

User Interface Defaults

User Interface Defaults allow you to specify defaults for regions and items. Using common user interface defaults promotes consistency, which makes your application easier to use, and likely to require less supporting documentation.

As of APEX 4, User Interface Defaults exist in two categories: the Table Dictionary and the Attribute Dictionary. The Table Dictionary contains defaults by table, for all the columns of the table. Table Dictionary defaults are usually initialized from the database definition and then customized as desired. The Attribute Dictionary, new in APEX 4, allows specification of defaults based on column names, and includes synonym features so that all columns of that name—no matter the source—will be assigned the same attributes. Attribute Dictionary settings may be initialized or updated from page items and report columns. You can also use the Attribute Dictionary to update page item and report column settings.

One process flow for populating the User Interface Defaults dictionaries is to use the Table Dictionary Synchronize function to populate defaults for tables and columns in your schema, and then migrate these settings to the Attribute Dictionary using the Attribute Dictionary Migration task. Migrating settings from the Table Dictionary to the Attribute Dictionary removes them from the Table Dictionary. Next, create some forms and reports, adjust the settings of various items as desired, and then update the Attribute Dictionary based on your customized page item and report column settings. Once your Attribute Dictionary is loaded, you can also use the Attribute Dictionary to update page items and report columns. How you initially populate and use the Table and Attribute Dictionaries is up to you. Note that defaults in the Table Dictionary will override any defined within the Attribute Dictionary, so be mindful to remove tables from the Table Dictionary when you have superseded those settings with Attribute Dictionary entries.

For example, synchronizing the Table Dictionary at the start of a project will set the default data types and populate all table and column comments. Figure 8-3 illustrates using the Table Dictionary Synchronize function. This is an easy way to load all your help text, since your data definition standards dictate that you have comments defined on your tables and columns. Once you have populated the Table Dictionary, when you create forms and reports, the table column attributes may be used by the APEX Create wizards. Be sure to select the Use User Interface Defaults option in the wizard—this ensures the attributes you have just set will get used.

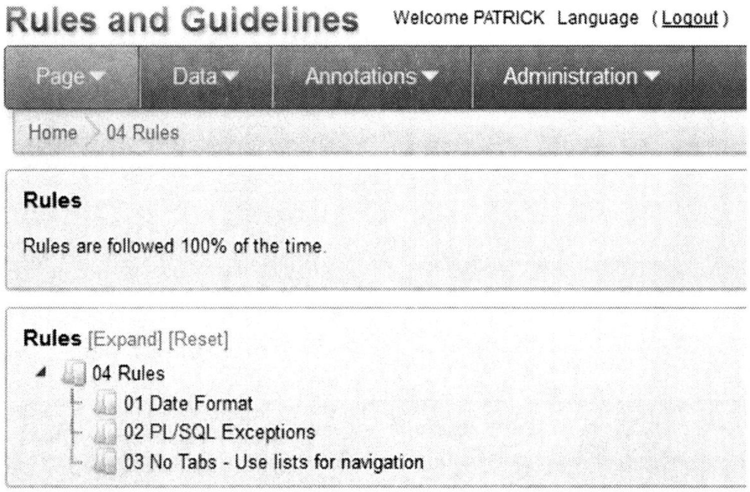

Figure 8-3. APEX User Interface Defaults, synchronizing the Table Dictionary with the schema

Figure 8-4 shows the Use User Interface Defaults option on the Create Form and Report wizard. If this option is not selected, your User Interface Defaults will not be applied.

Once you have created a form or report, the Attribute Dictionary detects when there are settings on the page that could be either loaded into the Attribute Dictionary, or updated on the page based on the settings in the Attribute Dictionary. Keeping the dictionary attributes synchronized with your page item and report column settings promotes a common look-and-feel throughout your application. This makes it easier for users to follow and easier for developers to maintain, and reduces the amount of supporting documentation that may be required. When your look-and-feel standards are included as User Interface Defaults, APEX actually helps you apply them throughout your application.

One way to easily bring existing database comments into the Attribute Dictionary is to create a simple form based on the table, and then update the Attribute Dictionary using the "Review items for update of the Attribute Dictionary" option and selecting the columns to update.

Figure 8-5 displays the Attribute Dictionary dashboard for a given APEX page, in this case, a form where we have 11 items for which the page attributes differ from the dictionary attributes.

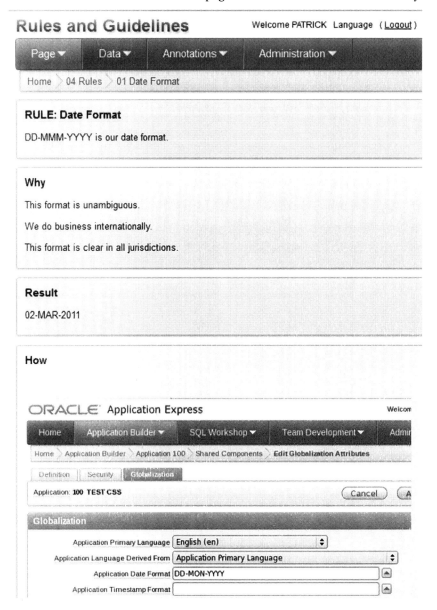

Figure 8-4. *Selecting the Use User Interface Defaults option in the Form and Report wizard*

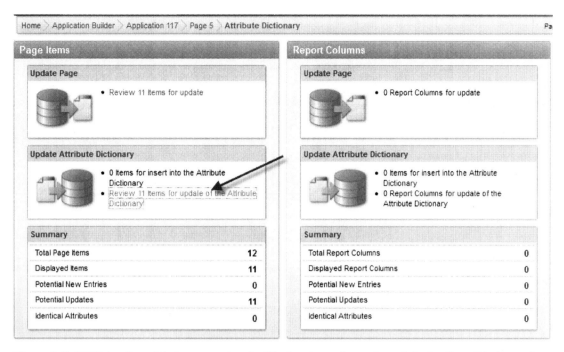

Figure 8-5. *APEX Attribute Dictionary, using the "Review items for update of the Attribute Dictionary" option*

Figure 8-6 shows the Update Attribute Dictionary interface. On this page, select the attributes to be added to the Attribute Dictionary, and click Update Attribute Dictionary. These attributes will now be applied in the next use of the Create Form or Create Form and Report wizard for those columns.

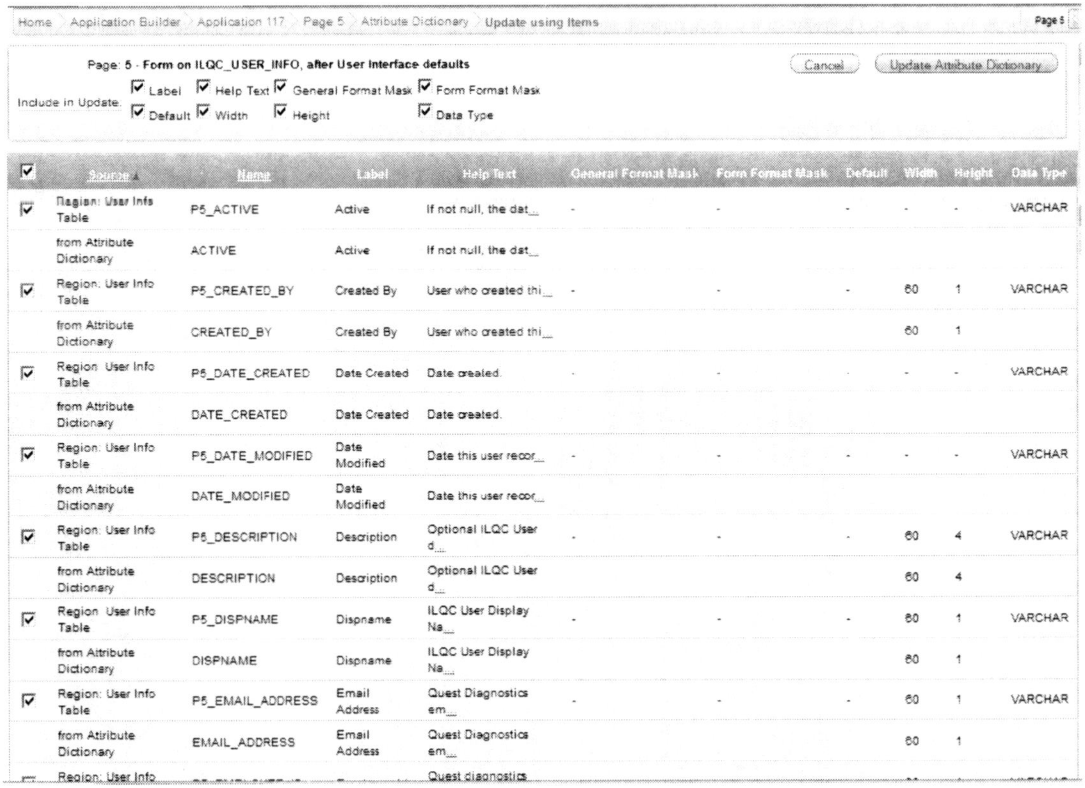

Figure 8-6. APEX Attribute Dictionary, using the Update Using Items interface

Alternatively, from the Attribute Dictionary dashboard, you could opt to update the items on your page with attributes in the Attribute Dictionary. To do so, select the option in the Update Page region, and then select the items to update on your page. Applied in either direction, this ability to synchronize item attributes is a huge timesaver that adds quality and consistency to your application.

End-User Documentation

User documentation for an APEX project may take many forms, but the least costly, most valuable documentation is often contained in user help text. User documentation in the form of help text should take the same format on every page. Individual item help, tooltips, or page help are all acceptable, as long as the mode of help is consistent across your application, and perhaps across an entire suite of applications. Users don't like change, and they don't like unexpected surprises. If all your interfaces operate on the same general flow and look-and-feel, user confidence is higher and user feedback is improved. We have just forwarded our working software while providing simple documentation at least cost. A win-win situation!

Remember the standard APEX help items must be updated by a developer. Changes to help text necessitate an application change—and a round through the promotion cycle from development to quality assurance to production. This is good if source control and change management are tied in with your promotion cycle. This can be costly if promotions are performed manually, and if there is a system of approvals and system change request tickets to go through.

If you need to make help changes independent of application changes—perhaps users are requesting additional details, or your data is evolving such that additional instruction is required, or an entirely separate department of business users handles the help and documentation content—consider using your own table to hold help text, and building your own help regions and pages. All you need do is design and build your help table, build an interface for maintaining the help data, and assign the business users access to the maintenance interface, and you now have help text that can be dynamically updated through the Help Maintenance interface, by the business (or whoever is authorized to use the new interface).

If we developers have done our job right in building an intuitive, web-based application that uses a familiar look-and-feel, includes item-, region-, and page-level help text as outlined in our standards, and follows all other rules and guidelines for our project, the need for additional end-user documentation should be minimal.

When additional end-user documentation is required—and there will come a time—remember our theme of "just enough." User tutorials may be necessary for more complicated forms or interfaces, or when specific formats or interfaces must be stipulated. When creating such documents, one suggestion is to make use of screenshots to create a pictorial step-by-step guide. A second suggestion is to build documents that can serve as both training manuals and reference documents, effectively cutting the documentation load in half. My opinion is that step-by-step tutorials are required only when the flow of the application is non-standard and non-intuitive. Your organization may mandate differently. In such cases, be sure to document and present the cost of building the documentation vs. the questionable value added. If you do need to document, do so only when the interface is finalized.

Developer Documentation

The point of developer documentation is to communicate to the next person (or yourself years later) how the application is built—the mechanical plumbing. Developer documentation for an APEX project includes the following:

- Following all naming standards

- Adding concise, meaningful comments in program code units: PL/SQL stored procedures, CSS files, JavaScript, and plug-ins, where applicable

- Religiously adding (and updating) developer comments

- Technical manuals only when absolutely necessary

Agile developer documentation begins with following guidelines and standards when building the application. Follow standards for naming conventions, page numbering, aliasing, region and item attributes, and the use of dynamic actions. Take advantage of plug-ins, where possible, for consistency of features, and to avoid duplication of code. All of these simple actions document your application because "this is how we do it." The consistency afforded by standards makes an application easier to follow and easier to learn and maintain.

Write code comments where necessary to explain major steps or unusual algorithms that may not be readily understandable. Follow your organization's standards for commenting (include dates, names, and ticket reference numbers). Comment with concise, accurate information as the code is developed. In APEX, where possible, use the developer comments. Developer comments are the entries in the Comments attribute of Page, Region, and Page Item elements. I am not saying to always add developer comments to every page, region, and item. That does not add value when the use of an item is obvious. I am recommending that you do add developer comments wherever necessary to explain a non-standard element or some special treatment, or to mark a change made for a bug fix. Those cases add value.

On occasions where a technical manual is either mandated or required due to some feature or complexity that needs more explanation than can be reasonably communicated in comments, write one. Be concise but thorough, and publish it in electronic format. My experience is that it is not necessary to document technical details of every item of every form and every report on every page (unless of course each of those items is used to interface with another system). It is necessary to document non-standard elements, non-standard feature usage or omissions, interesting security aspects, and anything that is not intuitively obvious to the next developer. Assume that your technical audience has both working knowledge of APEX and your subject matter, lest you end up in the task of writing an APEX manual (we already have a nice online one published by the APEX team) or a business document (which is better left to a subject matter expert). As a final note, do not write your technical documentation until your technical details are finalized, as late as possible.

System Documentation

Aside from the process documentation available through the APEX Utilities, system documentation should most notably include source control and change management. A good source control system—any source control system—serves as documentation of the evolution of your code base. The most important two words about source control are: Use it.

APEX application files, because they are database packages, do not readily lend themselves to traditional checkout-checkin-build source control systems. However, application files are just files, and can certainly be tracked with any source control system capable of handling files (which had better be all of them!). It takes just a little discipline to export from APEX and import into your source control system, consistently. Granted, this export/import process will seem like a big effort, until it becomes a habit.

In recent projects, I have successfully used CVS and Subversion to track all DDL, DML, APEX application files and supporting documents of all types. In these cases, all scripts were submitted to QA, and upon approval to production for DBAs to execute and install. The use of source control was mainly manual, but due to the small team and privileged promotion process, it worked. While not airtight, it was cost-effective in that situation.

A better system is to completely automate the promotion process by developing promotion scripts that handle schema changes (DDL), file updates (CSS and JS), and application installation. For an excellent example of a system-wide promotion process that covers all aspects of an APEX project, see Chapter 9 of *Expert Oracle Application Express*. The chapter was written by Dietmar Aust. It describes best practices and procedures for requirements management, file system layout, automated DDL extraction, script-based promotion system, and Subversion integration for APEX projects. It is likely that one or more of the components of the configuration and life cycle management system that Dietmar describes may make sense for your environment. My point is not to prescribe that system for everyone, but to point out what is possible regarding system management and change history. Given what is possible, apply the principles of Agile documentation to discern the right solution for your project. Do just enough.

The key is to balance essential source control and change management requirements for your project with the costs to implement them at your site. At minimum, a control and promotion process should include manual or automatic logging of the components updated when, by whom, and why. The "why" should track back to a specific requirement, enhancement request, or comment, which could be tracked in the Team Development tool, or some other change control system. Here is another area where the use of Team Development is a low-cost method of tracking system changes—relatively low-cost, valuable documentation of your application development history.

The source control requirements of course are heavier if the costs of system failure are higher. In that case, a larger investment in source control and change management is justified. My experience is that source control and change management are usually undervalued, until there is a failure. Any process, manual, automated, or some combination, adds value in ensuring recovery of your system and documentation of its history. If the costs of failure are higher, a greater investment in system documentation, including change history and source control, is justified.

No matter what system you implement, its use should become another habit.

Documentation for Business Users

Business users may need documentation that confirms implementation of the business rules, validates defined use cases, or confirms conformity to industry standards. In each of the cases, the working software is the best evidence. Videos that demonstrate operation of your application may suffice. If the documentation must be formal text on a page, consider integrating charts, diagrams, spreadsheets, images, and snippets of APEX interactive reports as opposed to plain text. Each of these visual modes of communication conveys information more quickly and efficiently than typed words.

Business users can also take advantage of Team Development information through the Team Development interactive reports. This is another case where Team Development incurs no cost other than data entry time, and yields valuable forms of documentation. This again promotes the core principles of simplicity and collaboration between the business and developers.

Business rules often need to be referenced or included as requirements in end-user or supporting documentation. When possible, strive to write the rules once, preferably into an online form, and generate reports from the stored data that communicate the desired business rule information. If business rules or use cases have been added as Team Development features, simple interactive reports on that data allow business users to pull the information they need when they need it. Business rules are apt to change over time, so there is value-added in creating a maintenance interface that also serves as an interactive report of your business rules repository. There is significantly less value and greater cost incurred in creating a Word document that must be maintained each time there is a business rule change, besides the fact that it pulls a developer away from writing code.

Trainers

If you have followed the principles of standard, Agile APEX development and produced simple, intuitive HTML pages, your training materials may be as simple as scripted how-to tutorials. Write one tutorial that covers the basic features of your application. Write additional tutorials for how to use more complicated, non-intuitive features. Gauge your writing to your audience. Non-technical users who are using their first online application will need more detailed instructions than a seasoned team of data entry users.

Test-drive your training materials as you develop them by working collaboratively with members of your audience. Can they follow the steps easily? Are you missing steps? Your audience can tell you, and it is best they do so during the documentation process so you can adjust your level of detail when necessary. Use screenshots, many of them, to document the application flow. Screenshots communicate the message more efficiently than exhaustive, step-by-step text descriptions of every action on every page. More complicated pages will of course need more detailed descriptions in the form of more screenshots. Always use clear, succinct text in active sentences. My recommendation is to prepare training documents that double as online tutorials and reference material, or vice versa. The point is to not double-document—with a little planning, one document can serve several purposes.

Do you need printed training documents? This is debatable and depends on the trainer and the application. Trainers need an agenda to follow. Trainees like to have some tangible material that documents their learning experience. Is the printed page the best medium? Not in all cases. My suggestion is to deliver training documents that also serve as user reference guides in online format. If users desire to print them, they can.

Summary

Agile documentation is the application of Agile software development principles to documenting aspects of your system that are not communicated otherwise. The concepts are simple: do only what is necessary, in the most effective mode of communication possible, at the least cost to the project relative to the value added. Agile documentation is clear, concise, direct, and to the point.

APEX includes products and features that facilitate Agile documentation. The APEX Utilities and Team Development tools offer out-of-the-box, low-cost opportunities to document aspects of your project. Creating and following standards as a natural part of the development process serve to minimize the amount of additional documentation that is required. The User Interface Defaults, help text, and developer comment features allow a developer to incorporate Agile documentation during the development process. The online, simple intuitive nature of APEX pages (when designed and built accordingly!) means documentation in the form of screenshots, videos, and other online tutorial formats is often sufficient for training and reference purposes. When mandated corporate or regulatory documentation is required, build only what is essential, in the most expedient method possible.

Above all remember that the fact that we are producing documentation does not mean we are abandoning or ignoring the value of face-to-face communication. The only valid reason to create documentation is to supplement and add value when other forms of communication are not possible or are insufficient for the purpose. When it is necessary to invest in documentation, plan for and do as little as possible, as efficiently as possible, as late as possible, and deliver just enough for your audience.

CHAPTER 9

Quality Assurance

Delivery of high-quality working software on a fast and regular basis is the goal of Agile software development. This book has discussed how to incorporate Agile practices in your APEX development process but so far has not specifically addressed quality. This chapter focuses on the principle of *continuous attention to technical excellence and good design.* And of course beyond pure *technical excellence and good design,* the software has to do what it is supposed to—not just be technically elegant. This chapter gives an overview of Agile quality assurance and then highlights APEX features and best practices to build quality into your application throughout the development and delivery process.

Agile Quality Assurance

In Agile software development, quality assurance is an integral part of the culture. Chapter 8 mentions applying standards until they become habits. Regarding quality, habits must become culture. Every team member is responsible for quality, and every team member is responsible for testing.

   This is a big change for those who are used to traditional waterfall development methods, where the ping-pong process of testing predominates:

> Serve finished code → Testers test
> ← Testers volley back bugs
> Developer fixes bugs → Testers test
> ← Testers pass back bugs
> Developer fixes bugs → Testers test
> ← Testers pass back bugs
> Developer fixes bugs → Testers test
> ← Testers pass back bugs
> and on and on …

   At some point in the game, someone runs out of bugs or fixes, or time's up and deployment happens. Each side focuses on clearing their list and tossing it back to the other team, but communication and collaboration between teams is not encouraged.

   At one site, we were told that no interaction between development and quality assurance was best, so that developers would not taint the testers. The net result was that the entire process took longer. At each volley, bugs and estimates and fixes were meticulously recorded; meetings tracked numbers, percents, graphs, and slopes; everyone was focused and stressed; and progress was slow but inevitable. We got there. Eventually Agile quality assurance is not like that.

   Agile quality assurance is the practice of building quality into every step of your design and development process. It is not a before or after action, it is a *during* action.

   Every member of the Agile team is responsible for quality, starting on day 1 and continuing through deployment. Customer, project manager, developer, business analyst, and yes, the quality assurance person all have an equal responsibility for quality, including testing. Each is equally tasked with answering the question, "Is our software working or not?" Testing is as much the responsibility of the developer as it is the business analyst or the tester or any other member of the Agile development team. All viewpoints are valuable and important to the process.

Agile quality assurance comes in many flavors, depending on the Agile methodology and the nature of the project and the organization. It is beyond the scope of this book to discuss them all, and it is not our intent to promote one over the other. However, several concepts are common to most Agile quality assurance viewpoints and are most certainly applicable to APEX quality assurance:

- Quality is a team culture. The whole team is responsible.

- Follow rules and guidelines.

- Create tests first. Know the answer to the question, "How do we know we are done?"

- Automate tests.

- Integrate continuously.

- Promote and use feedback.

The following sections address each of these points.

Quality as Culture

The whole team is responsible for quality assurance. *Close daily co-operation between business people and developers* throughout the process means that every team member, every day, has not just the chance but the responsibility to speak up and cooperate. Although it isn't an agenda item at every meeting, quality is an integral aspect of every sprint, every conversation, and every task. To ensure a quality end product, every team member needs to speak when something is not working as it should. This includes cases of

- It doesn't work as described. (Bug: let's fix it.)

- It works as described, but that's not what I meant. (Miscommunication: let's clarify what you meant.)

- It works as described, but I see now I really don't need that; I need this instead. (Discovery: let's build what you really need.)

- It works as described, but I don't need that sort of thing at all. (Throw away.)

It is common in Agile software development to encounter each of these cases. There is nothing right or wrong here; it is part of the process. The sooner these cases are flushed out, the better. The only way to flush them out is through constant communication between all members of the team. Code, demonstrate, and ask the question, "Are we done?" or, "Is this what you mean?" The key is for the team to accept this interaction and feedback as a normal process, adjust, and move on.

As a simple example, in Friday's Scrum meeting, I demonstrated the latest User Admin module. The security folks asked for a Y/N flag instead of a date for ease of querying. Managers need the date. Security wanted User Role added as a column. A business user wanted "Maintenance" instead of "Administration" or "Admin". We talked, settled on date and flag, agreed that "Maintenance" or "Maint" was fine for all, and added User Role. By the end of the 30-minute call, the changes were in place. Done. On to the next task. Oh yes: they need a Login Failures page from which they can restore logins. Got it;

it's ready for Monday's meeting. Everyone pointed out their needs, the developer was not mortally offended by any of it, consensus was reached quickly, changes were implemented and demonstrated, and everyone went back to work. Face-to-face (well, Net Meeting) communication accomplished in under 30 minutes what could have been days. That's Agile.

This is not to say every member of the team must have a testing background or a quality assurance background. In reality, team member expertise will overlap. Regarding testing and quality, a customer brings a different perspective to testing than does a developer, a business analyst, or the project manager. The customer is looking for usability: they want to get their work done. The business analyst is looking to ensure that a business process is complete. The project manager is looking to sign off on a task or create a new one. The developer's brain may be stuck behind the code and less focused on the user interface. All perspectives are needed. It is the overlapping of skill sets and perspectives that adds value.

Note that a key part of this culture is trust. Team members must trust that their word will be heard, that they are an equal with every other member of the team, and that collaboration is open and unmeasured. There are no negative consequences for pointing out cases of "It works as described, but I don't need that anymore." If your team cannot develop this trust, then your process will be hampered (at best), or it will fail.

If one or more team members is stubborn or indecisive, your process will be hampered—talking points will not be settled in one meeting or will require longer meetings. Longer and subsequent meetings take time (resources) and may necessitate extending the project schedule (more resources). Such indecision can quickly become expensive. In APEX, development is fast, and developers can quickly move on to the next task. Missing bugs or issues, minor or major, early in the development process due to fear of embarrassment or ego-bruising negatively affects the quality of the software. When team dynamics break down, software quality suffers. This point is not unique to Agile software development; it is just more painfully noticeable. There must be trust for there to be an environment that promotes true quality. Your team must be a team, and quality must be part of the culture.

Build Quality into Rules and Guidelines

Rule and guidelines serve to improve code quality. For example, the technical design standard of following third normal form for relational integrity promotes solid database design. Good database design promotes good data. A guideline of separating business logic from presentation logic makes an application easier to debug and test, among other values. The topic of rules and guidelines is addressed in Chapter 3.

Create Tests First

Before developing anything, before starting any task, the team needs to know, "How do we know we are done?" That question is best answered with this one: "How do we test it?" The team may need to collaborate on how best to test certain features or tasks. At these times, the process of defining the test serves to clarify the task. At minimum, team members need to agree on the test success criteria, because this is what answers the "How do we know we are done?" question. This is what tells you when you're "done".

The practice of test-driven development involves building tests, usually true/false assertions, to validate requirements before coding, and then adjusting and expanding the tests as development evolves. The premise is that to write a test, the developer must completely understand the requirement. The Agile team works together to define and agree on the test, thus clarifying the task at hand. Developers need write only enough code to pass the test, following the Keep It Simple Stupid (KISS) and You Ain't Gonna Need It (YAGNI) principles. In this way, test-driven development, and variations of this practice, serve to keep development lean and focused, serving the end goal of delivering working software.

Remember that testing a web application involves testing for several aspects, not just a simple true/false "it works or it doesn't." When you're planning tests, consider testing that covers all these areas:

- *Functionality:* Do all the items, pages, links, and images work? Is all business logic correct? Does the HTML/CSS validate? Are all database interactions correct?

- *Usability:* Is the application simple and intuitive to operate? Are all features operable? Is content clear? Is help readily accessible?

- *Interface:* Are all database and application server interactions as designed?

- *Compatibility:* Does your application work in all supported browsers? On all operating systems? What about mobile clients? Do all charting and printing operations operate on all browsers and platforms?

- *Performance:* Does the application perform well under data load? Under user load? Do all page operations perform as expected?

- *Security:* Are all protected pages and processes protected? Is data secured? Are web directories accessible when they should be locked down? Do manual URL changes allow access to privileged operations?

This list is by no means comprehensive. The point is to think about what type of tests, and what depth of tests, are essential for your application. These questions are food for thought in developing your own test plan to cover your application.

Automate Tests Where Possible

Each story or module should include a task for unit-test development. Following the "Create tests first" point, this task should be early in the cycle, before coding. The cost of that task should be in proportion to the size and complexity of your deliverable. Over time, you will have a suite of unit-test scripts. As your test suite grows, it only makes sense to automate the execution of these tests, to save time, to save effort, for repeatability, and to not disrupt current and future development. Strive for *working software delivered frequently.* If the team spends more time testing, they are doing less development, and they are delivering less useful software less frequently. It's simple: spend as little time testing as possible. Do just enough (sound familiar?) to be effective and repeatable. Balance the cost of building the tests with the return on investment.

As of this writing, there are no automated test suites tailored specifically for APEX development. We suspect that will change in the near future. There are, however, several automated test products that assist in testing PL/SQL program units and in testing web application screens. A combination of these types of products can cover both the business logic (the PL/SQL modules) and the presentation logic (the page flow and operation) of your APEX application.

For PL/SQL unit testing, consider products like SQL Developer PL/SQL Unit Testing, Quest Code Tester for Oracle, utPLSQL (the precursor to Quest Code Tester), DbFit, and others that may be embedded in your favorite PL/SQL integrated development environment (IDE).

For scripting web-application page flow, consider products like Selenium. Selenium is an open source suite of tools for testing web applications. The Selenium IDE has a recording feature that records user actions and saves them as a reusable script that can later be executed to validate an application's operation. Many commercial products provide similar functionality.

Also consider scripting for life-cycle management: for promoting your application from development to your testing environment to production, conditional on passing an automated suite of acceptance or regression tests. Chapter 9 of *Expert Oracle Application Express* (Apress, 2011) describes a proven approach for testing and the promotion process.

The one exception to the "Automate tests" principle is when your application and the tests to validate it are so simple that the process of automating those tests would take more time than running them repeatedly manually. In that case, do not waste resources automating. Tests are important—they reduce bugs and eliminate waste. Take care not to introduce waste when building your tests.

Above all, keep your tests as simple as possible. We have seen incredibly beautiful and complex test worksheets that record every test and quantify results through charts and graphs. This is wonderful, but how much time did it take away from development? Unless you have a requirement to formally document test suites and test results, restrain from spending as much time developing tests as you do developing your application. No one cares how elegant your test scripts are. They do care that your software works.

Continuous Integration

Continuous integration is a core Agile practice. The principle *Continuous attention to technical excellence and good design* reminds you that you are continually integrating quality. *Close, daily cooperation between business people and developers* means you are integrating code frequently, preferably on a daily basis (or more frequently), so that business users and developers can communicate about whether it works. If it works, you move on. If it doesn't, you fix it now.

Feedback, Feedback, Feedback

Feedback is essential to Agile software development, no less so where quality is concerned. The principle of *Close daily cooperation between business people and developers* encourages interactions. Feedback—information exchange—ensures that the team stays on the target of producing quality working software. Feedback allows the team to know when it is not on target, and to adapt as needed. Feedback makes the entire Agile development concept work. Without it, the team is proceeding (or not) blindly. The delivery of quality working software suffers.

Team members should partake in honest, open exchanges, stating early and clearly when code is not producing results or is producing unintended results. All team members should learn to ask questions to draw out feedback when it is not forthcoming. As a developer, ask if the customer's needs are being met. As a customer, ask if the programmers have enough information to begin coding. Ask these questions in planning meetings and retrospectives as well as at scheduled daily meetings.

Feedback can take many forms—verbal or written, formal or informal. E-mail, voicemail, sketches, video, phone calls, drawings, instant messages, text messages, notes, spreadsheets, and documents are all valid forms of feedback. Whenever possible, make feedback visible to all team members. Preserve feedback only if it is essential to document the progression of the project. When feedback must be preserved, do so in the most efficient mode possible. The point is to enable and encourage open information exchange toward improving the software product. Successful Agile software development doesn't just happen: it only happens because the interactions between team members enable it. Collaborative feedback throughout the lifecycle of the product is essential.

APEX Features for Quality Assurance

APEX incorporates many tools for quality assurance, ranging from the application builder wizards to the Debug Repository to the full suite of APEX application utilities. The following sections highlight the more useful APEX tools and utilities that promote the concepts of building in quality and validating that it exists during the development process. A more complete treatment of each of these tools can be found in the APEX documentation.

Wizards

You may not normally think of development wizards as a quality assurance tool, but think again. The APEX wizards create all the elements required for the object being created. For a simple form on a table or view, that means page items; validations; fetch, insert, update, and delete processes; buttons; and branches. Add a report on the same table, and the wizard also creates navigational elements for moving between pages and the report, including all default report column, pagination, and search settings. You *can* build those elements manually and produce the same result, but why? Using the wizard ensures that everything is created exactly as it should be, with no mistakes. The wizard enables error-free development of moderately complex components in a matter of seconds. That not only promotes quality but also economizes on development time.

When an APEX wizard is available, use it. It is most always more economical to use a wizard and customize the result as needed than it is to build from scratch. The result is fewer typos, fewer mistakes, and faster time to working software. That's what you want.

User Interface Defaults

User Interface Defaults promote a common look, feel, and operation of page items and report columns, and minimize developer time spent individually setting element attributes. Commonality looks professional and makes your end users happy because the look and operation of your application is consistent.

User Interface Defaults allow a developer to synchronize page-item and column settings with underlying table and column settings, using the Table Dictionary or the Attribute Dictionary, for propagation of those settings to like page items and columns. You save time in both cases. User Interface Defaults and the Table and Attribute Dictionaries are discussed in greater detail in Chapter 8.

Unit Testing

Gotcha. There is no APEX-supplied unit-testing framework. This section is here to remind you that even though APEX does not currently include a unit-testing module, unit tests need to be created and executed, the sooner the better in the development cycle.

User Acceptance Tests

Gotcha again. APEX has no built-in tool for acceptance tests. The recommendation is to use the same methodology used for unit and regression tests, *plus* ad-hoc testing by real users.

In our opinion, user acceptance testing (UAT) is mandatory. At some point during development, team members become too close to the code and the product for unbiased acceptance testing. They know too well how the code is supposed to work, and they know all the exception cases built into the unit tests, but they are not end users and just don't have the uncanny ability to find a bug no matter what. End users have that knack. Certain end users excel at it. Make note of the bug-finding, gifted end users, because they are your best friends (or your worst enemies) when it comes to UAT time.

Acceptance tests don't just execute the unit test suites again. UAT must include users exercising the system as they will normally be using it. Normal use is not scripted—it involves all kinds of unexpected clicks, starts, stops, and hiccups that most testing teams do not plan for.

Acceptance tests are best done just after successful unit tests, at the end of each sprint, when features of the functionality just developed are fresh in the development team's mind. Yes, performing acceptance tests means there will be some overlap as issues from the previous sprint in UAT must be dealt with while the next sprint is underway. This small amount of overlap is far preferable to waiting until the end of development, when discovering an error will be more costly. Errors found at the end of development are always more costly—we have yet to find an exception to that axiom. If time spent addressing issues found in UAT becomes significant, add a catch-up task to bring the project back on track.

If you have built and saved your unit tests, they need to be executed as part of or just prior to UAT. The key thing about UAT is the *user* part—have real live users test your application the way they, the real live users, will use it. It's just common sense to do so, but in many cases—and we're sure you know a few—it doesn't get done.

Acceptance tests are of course more critical for rocket science O-ring monitoring than for a three-page application that manages the in-office soccer pool. That only means the amount of time spent on unit tests and user acceptance tests for more critical applications is appropriately longer than for less critical applications. Excellence is the goal in both cases, balanced with the cost of attaining it and the cost of not attaining it.

APEX Debugging Tools

Although it isn't usually considered a quality assurance tool, the APEX debug module certainly promotes quality assurance by making it easier for the developer to deliver working code. The APEX team has provided a sizeable suite of debug mechanisms and approaches for tracking and solving most APEX errors and performance issues. Tools for code instrumentation, reports on page-rendering and page-processing events, an interactive debug mode, and a whole suite of APEX utilities to view debug information are a few of the APEX-supplied debugging options.

The Debug Repository records a wealth of information about the session state and page-rendering processes at the time of the bug. This information is invaluable for tracking errors and leads to addressing them more quickly. Faster debug time means faster delivery of working software. And that is the point: to deliver high-quality software quickly. Debugging in APEX is covered extensively in Chapter 6 of *Expert Oracle Application Express*. This is a recommended read for any developer building an APEX application.

APEX Advisor

The APEX Advisor, new in APEX 4.0, is APEX application quality assurance central. The Advisor is a utility that scans your APEX application for a select series of known best practice and value-added practices and reports when and exactly where your application falls short. It sounds a bit intimidating, and in fact it can be. It's a health check. Run the Advisor, and it tells you exactly what and where in your application you are not following the selected quality criteria. The Advisor report includes links to the offending page, so you can readily correct the deficiency.

Access the APEX Advisor from the Application Builder Utilities menu. Figure 9-1 shows this menu, including the Advisor option.

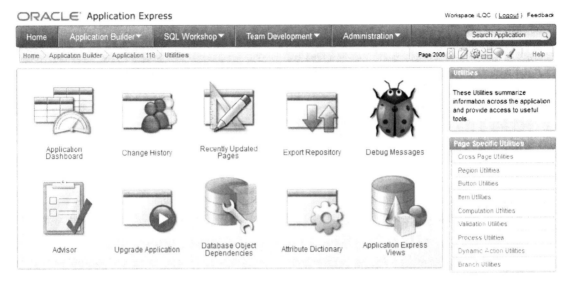

Figure 9-1. Accessing the APEX Advisor through the APEX Utilities menu

---

Note While at the APEX Utilities menu, take note of all the options: Application Dashboard, Change History, Recently Updated Pages, Export Repository, Debug Messages, Upgrade Application, Database Object Dependencies, Attribute Dictionary, and Application Express Views. Each of these is a view or report on your application in its current state or recent history. Each utility offers valuable information for a specific purpose. These utilities are a window into the metadata that APEX maintains on the development and execution of your application pages. This information is often useful in tracking and recovering from errors or for improving performance.

The Advisor interface allows you to select which checks to perform and a list of pages to check. Checks fall into these categories:

- Errors
- Security
- Warnings
- Performance
- Usability
- Quality Assurance

Each check has a tooltip that contains a brief explanation of what the check does. Not all checks make sense for all applications. Determining which make sense for your application and your organization may take a few tries. Don't be intimidated—all of these checks add value, yet some of them may seem picky. Only you can decide if it is essential to address all of them. The checks applied should coincide with the standards documented in your rules and guidelines. Our recommendation is to at minimum address all errors and security failures. Figure 9-2 shows the Advisor Check to Perform and Check Pages elements. Figure 9-3 shows a sample Advisor results page.

On the Advisor Results page, you can filter the results by check to narrow the scope of results for ease in addressing them. To address a failed check, simply click the View link at the bottom of the listing to navigate to the page of the failed check. Once there, resolve the issue, and you are one step closer to quality.

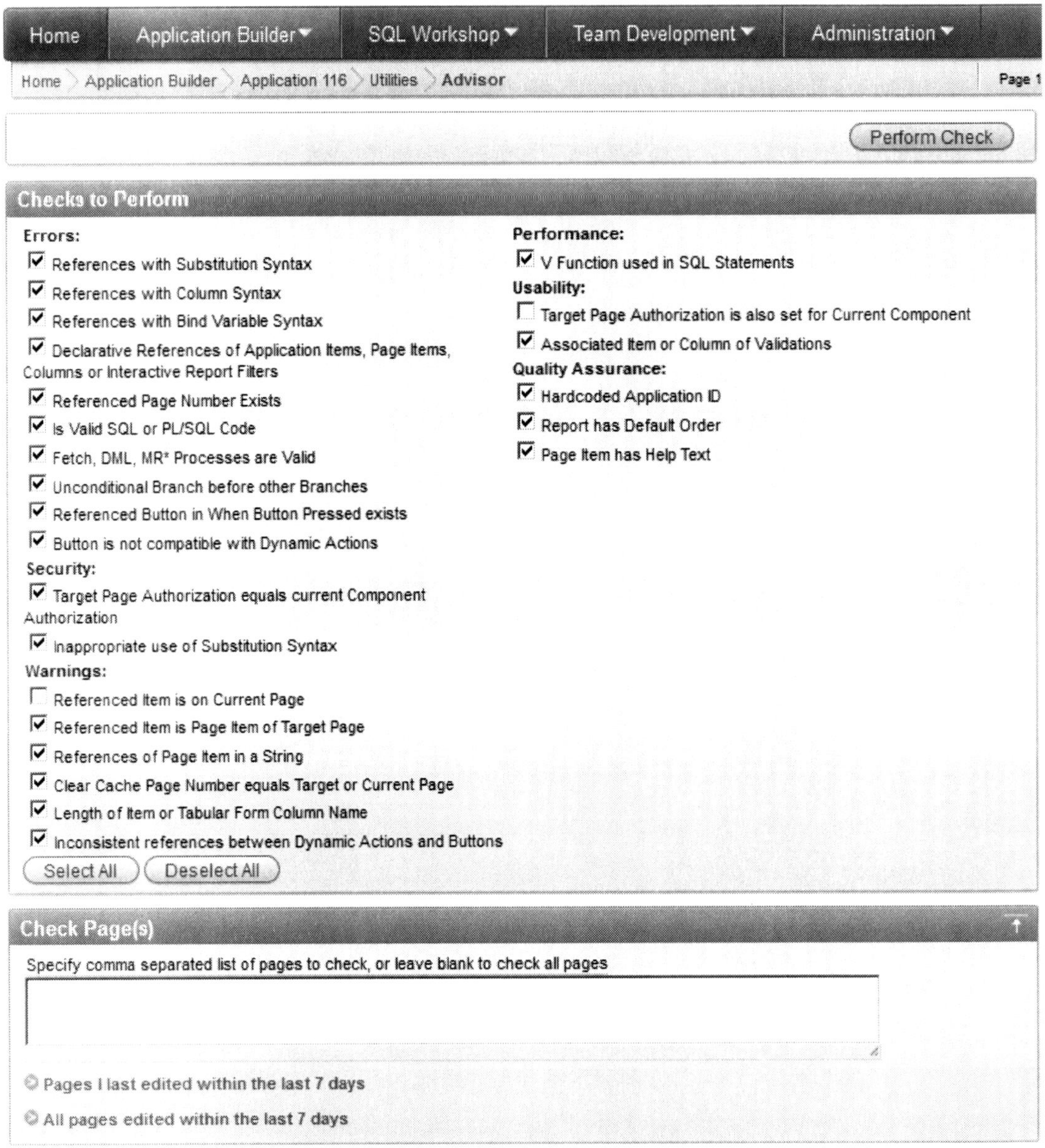

Figure 9-2. APEX Advisor: selecting checks to perform, and Check Page(s)

Applications > 116 - ILQC > Pages > 0 - 0 > Regions > Data Management Options	
Attribute	Condition Expression1 (Specifies an expression based on the specific condition type selected.)
Check	Referenced Page Number Exists
Category	Error
Message	Page 2000 does not exist.
Value	2000,2002,2004,2006,2008,2010,2012,2014,2016,2018,2020,2022,2024,2026,2028,2030,2032
	View

Figure 9-3. Advisor result

Team Development

The Team Development module, discussed in detail in Chapter 6, offers Feedback, Milestones and Releases, Features, Bugs, and To Do's. Each of these modules facilitates communication and efficiency, key values in the Agile process. The Team Development utilities promote quality because they facilitate the Agile development process. Of these, the Feedback and Bugs modules are the most pertinent to quality assurance; but they all play a part in keeping the team organized, keeping developers on schedule, and tracking project features, bugs, and enhancements. Whether you use one or a combination of these modules, the simple, lightweight Team Development framework is wise addition to an Agile APEX development project. The following sections supplement Chapter 6, with a focus on quality assurance.

Feedback

One of the most obvious modes of quality assurance in APEX is the Team Development Feedback utility. The Feedback module is invaluable for immediate, complete, documented communication among all members of the team. Such communication enhances the Agile process and thereby improves quality. The under-the-hood values automatically captured by the Feedback module enable thorough analysis of the issues and comments entered. This information is essential for bug tracking, because you cannot count on getting it from your users. It is a common phenomenon for end users to loudly declare, "It doesn't work," "I got an error," or "It's broken," and yet have absolutely no recall of any additional details, such as *what* didn't work, what error message they saw, or *how* it's broken. The highly motivated members of your development team may be excellent, but they are not mind readers. Feedback is essential, however you can get it. The extra values that APEX passes on automatically are invaluable.

In a recent Agile project, we encountered a web interface error that was initially reported by only one user. The user passed on screenshots of the problem. The developer was unable to reproduce the error in any browser; the project manager was unable to produce the error in the standard IE 8 browser; and an on-site team developer was unable to reproduce the error. When the bug was reported in UAT of another application, the team realized the issue had to be addressed. But how could they address it if it couldn't be reproduced? The developer dove in and spent hours researching such behavior, examining the theme, the pages templates, and all custom CSS and HTML, basically searching for possible causes. He finally traced the issue to the use of IE 7 compatibility mode, with IE 7 document standards. Had this issue been reported with Feedback, the extra information regarding the reporter operating system and browser settings would have been available. Having this information would have saved hours of development time—the IE7 browser would have stood out as non-standard for the corporation. The development time and team brainpower in researching this problem was lost. The less tangible but perhaps more significant loss was in credibility. How could the developers deliver such buggy code? Customers do not expect—or deserve—significant user interface bugs, and first impressions are lasting, even in a development or test environment. Eventually the issue was resolved and credibility was restored, but the loss of any hour in an Agile project is significant. In this case, the lost time amounted to the equivalent of an entire task. That's the loss of a deliverable!

Our advice is to use the most efficient tools available to capture as much feedback (data) as possible as easily as possible. There is no doubt that the APEX Feedback utility is one of those efficient, useful, easy tools. For a developer, it is like feedback heaven delivered to your feet. Just pick it up and use it!

Note that not all users have access to Feedback by default. Non-developer, non-APEX Administrator team members must have access to APEX to be able to use it. It is possible to have Team Development–only APEX users: create a user who is not a developer and not an Administrator, and select Yes for Team Development Access. Make the appropriate selections in the Create User interface, in the Account Privileges region, as shown in Figure 9-4. Your feedback moderator may be one such user.

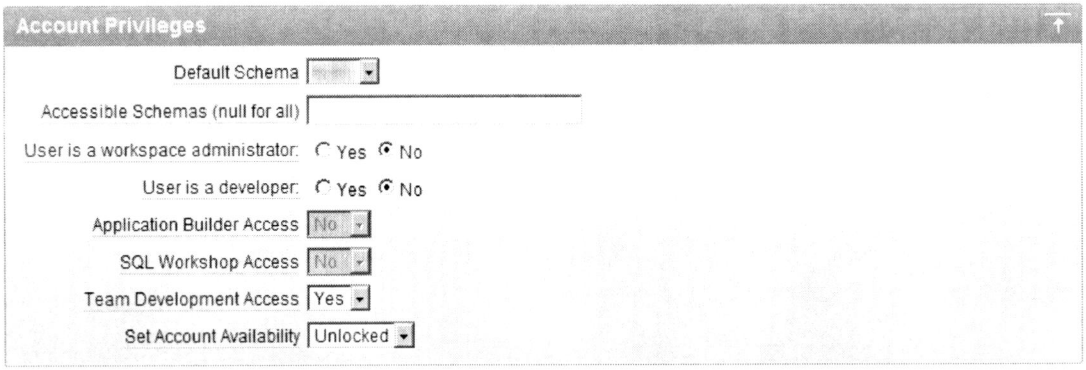

Figure 9-4. Setting account privileges for a Team Development–only user

Consider also that not every enterprise will embrace the use of Feedback and/or the Team Development module in general. There may be a corporate issue-tracking and change-management system, or something as simple as Microsoft Excel spreadsheets that are embedded in corporate culture and are the preferred manner of issue tracking. In these cases, team members can still use Feedback to rapidly enter issues as they are encountered. The feedback moderator can then download the feedback settings into the corporate issue-tracking system. The problem with this approach is that it is one-way—there is no "Import Feedback" utility for tracking responses to feedback items that are external to APEX. Once exported, the Feedback loop is interrupted. Our advice in these cases is to demonstrate the value of Feedback and the other Team Development features, emphasizing the value added versus the resource cost (how much time does it take you to maintain issues in the corporate system versus through APEX Team Development?). Of course, this value-add needs to be weighed across all team members, not just the developer.

The Feedback form is a plain-old APEX form page. This entire form may be customized as desired, following corporate development practices, of course. The Feedback module allows for up to eight custom fields that may be added to the Feedback pop-up form. These let you capture data or settings specific to your application or user environment. The point is to get information from the user to the development team, and vice versa, with the least pain possible and the least impact to the goal of delivering working software.

Bugs

The Bugs module is another important feature for Agile quality assurance. Feedback that is classified as a bug is automatically tracked within the Team Development network. Bugs can be tied to a release and assigned to a developer, who in turn closes the bug when it is completed. Although the Bugs module is not as complete as many off-the-shelf issue-tracking programs, for APEX development it is sufficient and lightweight, and it does the job. This follows the Agile practice of doing just enough, and no more.

It is up to your team to decide whether Team Development provides all the issue-tracking features and documentation required for your project or your enterprise. Remember that the APEX development team used Team Development in developing APEX 4, demonstrating that the Bugs module certainly contains the essentials for tracking issues in a sizeable APEX project.

Summary

Agile quality assurance is a *during* action—it occurs during the development process and is the responsibility of all team members, at every phase of the project. Although there are many approaches to ensuring quality in Agile software development projects, they all include these aspects:

- Instill quality as part of the culture.
- Follow rules and guidelines.
- Create tests first.
- Automate tests wherever possible.
- Integrate continuously.
- Promote and use feedback.

APEX provides many built-in tools for building quality into an application, all of which are free and completely integrated with the APEX instance. These tools include the create wizards in the Application Builder, the Debug Repository, the Team Development suite of tools, and the APEX utilities, highlighted by the APEX Advisor. In many cases, data is automatically collected by the APEX engine, as with the Feedback interface and debug mode. In other tools, such as Team Development milestones and To Do's, minimal user input is required.

Although APEX does not include built-in unit-test and acceptance-test modules, commercial and open source options are readily available for PL/SQL and web application testing that integrate well with APEX development. Because the end goal of your project is to deliver quality working software, it makes sense to adopt as many of these tools as practical to streamline the development process.

CHAPTER 10

Summary

Agile is a process. APEX is a tool. These two inanimate things are brought to life and blossom in the hands of skilled and motivated software developers.

Agile software development was conceived in the 1990s. It was born in 2001 when the Agile Manifesto and its 12 underlying principles were written and published. Agile's phenomenal uptake at the time was due to the software industry's hunger for a new approach to governing software development projects; the classical project management techniques that grew up in hard industries like construction did not work in the software industry. The failure of classical project management techniques in the software industry was due to the extremely fast pace of change in the software industry and the inherent malleability of software itself. Agile explicitly recognizes that hardware is hard and software is soft.

Agile software development values "*responding to change over following a plan.*" This is an important Agile value; however, Agile recognizes that the plan has value. Professional sports teams spend a huge amount of time practicing plays; plays are their plans. Successful execution of a play means success, so there is a huge incentive to devise and execute successful plays. A hard fact is that playing in a game is much different than practicing. In a game, there is an opposing team, there is a loud crowd making on-field communication difficult, the weather is always a factor, and then there is adrenaline flowing in the veins of each player. In this environment, many plays get broken. Highly successful teams are good at both executing planned plays and at scrambling to make the best of broken plays. When a play is broken, the team falls back on secondary and tertiary plans; if they are not an option, the players react and fall back on their individual training and conditioning to read the situation and respond. Championship teams excel at both executing planned plays and turning broken plays into successes. Agile software development explicitly recognizes this reality in the software industry by breaking a large project down into small iterations so that after each iteration, the team can evaluate its position and adjust to its current environment, which is often different than expected. Agile, in sporting terminology, means being quick on your feet.

Oracle Application Express (APEX) is a tool that is well suited for working in an Agile software development environment. The primary reason for the good fit is APEX's declarative architecture. Almost all of its core features can be implemented by stepping through point-and-click wizards that build complete web pages that are intimately tied to an underlying Oracle database. All of the tedious insert, select, update, and delete SQL statements are handled behind the scenes by the APEX engine, leaving the developer free to deal with the business rules that are associated with the page.

The fundamental building block in an APEX application is a web page. APEX web pages are generally built within a short amount of time, making it relatively easy to break an APEX application down into small units of useful functionality, which are delivered within short iterations of two to three weeks. This strategy fits extremely well with Agile software development.

"Out of the box" APEX is a powerful and efficient software development tool. Like all tools, it has strengths and weaknesses. The weaknesses are addressed by enhancing APEX through using supporting technologies. For example, APEX has no built-in print engine for producing formatted reports. BI

Publisher, PL/PDF, and Jasper Reports can be linked to APEX to fulfill this role. APEX applications that need a rich web environment may need the help of JavaScript libraries like jQuery and Ext JS. Enhancing APEX is often required to meet user expectations and to fulfill complicated requirements. Of course, enhancing APEX with external supporting technologies comes with a price: the tool becomes somewhat less Agile. This is due to a number of factors. The enhanced skill set that is required to implement the technologies forces your team to learn how to use the technologies or acquire new personnel with the requisite skills. There are more moving parts associated with your enhanced APEX application; risk is increased together with the cost of ongoing maintenance. More time is required to build and test the application. In general, when a team enhances APEX with supporting technologies, it must also move from a lightweight project governance model to a slightly heavier model; please realize that this can be done within an Agile software development environment.

The APEX "box" has grown significantly since its first major release as HTMLDB 1.5. Each major release has seen more and more external functionality being pulled into the APEX environment. For example, a lot of tedious hand-coded JavaScript is no longer necessary now that dynamic actions have been incorporated into APEX 4.x.

Does Agile software development ignore classical project management? No, it actually complements it. The only significant aspect of classical project management that Agile rebels against is a waterfall approach, in which detailed requirement gathering and design are done up front before construction begins. Waterfall, in a software development environment, fails in many cases. Agile promotes a strategy in which high-level planning is done at the beginning of a project. Detailed design is done in a "just in time" manner, in which it is left to individual iterations.

Agile software development respects the five project management process groups and the nine project management knowledge areas that are put forward in the Project Management Institute's (PMI) *A Guide to the Project Body of Knowledge (PMBOK Guide)*. This complementary relationship between Agile and PMI's view of project management has been formally recognized by PMI's introduction in 2011 of the PMI Agile Certified Practitioner (PMI-ACP) certification.

Oracle's APEX development team values Agile project governance and Agile project management. This fact is clearly demonstrated by the introduction of the Team Development module in APEX 4.0. Team Development is a lightweight project governance tool. It adheres to the Agile principle of "*simplicity.*" Team Development's elegant design makes it simple, extensible, and flexible; all of these attributes make it a good fit with Agile. The Features entity enables the team to capture and document a high-level plan for executing a project. Milestones organize the iterations by tracking release dates and the Features that are released with the iteration output. To Dos are used to help keep individual iterations on track; they are the tasks that are assigned to individual team members. Bugs track issues that are found by testers and end users; bugs, depending on their complexity, can be promoted to individual To Dos or Features. The Feedback mechanism pulls all of the stakeholders together by giving them an efficient way of recording any issue that they find with an APEX application. Feedback supports, in a big way, Agile's principle of "*close, daily co-operation between business people and developers.*" The existence of Team Development is a sure sign that APEX is rapidly maturing into a serious contender in the software development world.

Rules and guidelines, in an Agile software development context, are an effective format that can be used to efficiently capture a software development team's standards. Software development standards are key to adhering to Agile's principle of "*continuous attention to technical excellence and good design.*" Often, teams get bogged down by writing standards in a verbose and wordy manner; this is very un-Agile. The rules and guidelines format that is recommended in this book gives developers a concise and very terse way of capturing their standards in a format that is easy to write and maintain. APEX's Websheet module is an ideal authoring and publication mechanism for rules and guidelines. In a websheet, the rules and guidelines are easily accessible at all times to all of the developers. The websheet saves paper and is the single source of truth. At the end of each iteration, the results from the team's reflective iteration review can quickly be captured in the websheet version of the rules and guidelines and are ready to go at the beginning of the next iteration.

The Agile Manifesto values "*working software over comprehensive documentation*"; however, documentation has value and, in some regulated industries, is mandatory. Out of the box, APEX provides a number of ways to capture documentation within APEX's Application Builder. APEX also provides a number of ways to extract and publish the documentation. The exact way a team documents its applications and APEX environment can be defined in its rules and guidelines document or websheet. The trick is to minimize the number of documentation artifacts to keep the documentation effective yet lightweight. Well-crafted working software can be self-documenting to a large extent; however, a few snippets of well-crafted and accessible documentation can save a lot of time and grief when it is time to maintain the software or explain to users how and why it works the way it does.

We are software developers; building quality software is one of our professional passions. This passion is embodied in one of the most important Agile principles: "*continuous attention to technical excellence and good design.*" Applying this principle to our daily work is daunting because the word "quality" means many things to many people. We can, however, deal with quality by first defining it through another Agile principle, "*close, daily co-operation between business people and developers.*" The initial theoretical definition is usually articulated in a product's requirements document; the definition is then refined, if necessary, by adapting the theoretical definition to the practical needs of the individual product and customer.

Quality has two aspects:

- Quality must, in fact, exist in the product.

- Stakeholders need assurance that, in fact, the quality does exist.

"*Self-organizing teams*" define quality through their rules and guidelines. Rules and guidelines ensure that the software is constructed in a consistent and well-defined manner. APEX plays a part in this by providing a robust declarative environment that helps developers build applications whose mechanical workings are extremely reliable.

APEX can give the stakeholders good assurance that the software is built to high-quality standards. APEX applications are defined using metadata in the Oracle database. APEX provides many useful views of this metadata through its rich set of utilities, which includes a debug repository and the APEX Advisor. The views of the metadata provide useful tests for quality. Testing tools are not yet part of the APEX development environment; however, there are a number of testing tools available that work well with APEX.

Both authors of this book have been working almost exclusively with APEX for well over six years. In that time, we have had the pleasure of working with a wonderful group of people, the APEX developer community, who truly live by the sentiment that is expressed in the Agile Manifesto's opening line, "*We are uncovering better ways of developing software by doing it and helping others do it.*"

Index

■ C

CPSIA information can be obtained at www.ICGtesting.com
Printed in the USA
LVOW130241080312

272144LV00003B/60/P